COLLECTED
POEMS

# COLLECTED
# POEMS

BY
*Elder Olson*

THE UNIVERSITY OF CHICAGO PRESS
*Chicago & London*

# Phoenix Poets

*This book is also available in a clothbound edition from*
THE UNIVERSITY OF CHICAGO PRESS

*ISBN: 0-226-62915-5 (clothbound); 0-226-62914-7 (paperbound)*

*Library of Congress Catalog Card Number: 63-22589*

THE UNIVERSITY OF CHICAGO PRESS, CHICAGO 60637
The University of Chicago Press, Ltd., London

FOR MY CHILDREN
ANN
ELDER
OLIVIA
SHELLEY

# AUTHOR'S NOTE

This is a volume of Collected Poems in the sense that it is a gathering, not of everything I ever wrote, but of representative pieces from my first four volumes, together with more recent work. Part I contains poems from *Thing of Sorrow;* Part II, from *The Cock of Heaven;* Part III, from *The Scarecrow Christ;* Part IV, from *Plays and Poems, 1948–58.* Part V contains the recent poems, hitherto uncollected.

In composing *The Cock of Heaven,* I sought to make a long philosophic poem, constructed for the most part out of independent shorter ones, dealing with the history and nature of man and certain moral problems, as well as problems of guilt and innocence. These were presented in the form of the scholastic method: statement of question, division of question, argument and counterargument. To emphasize the permanence of the problems, I thought it might be effective to represent different voices discussing them in all ages, in a kind of simultaneous colloquy. This device necessitated the use of quotation both overt and hidden, allusion, and frequently direct imitation. I have chosen to break up the single long poem, salvaging parts which still interested me; and I offer this note to explain the technique of the poems of Part II.

# ACKNOWLEDGMENT

All but a few of the poems in Part V of this volume originally appeared in magazines, and for permission to reprint them here the author wishes to thank the editors of the following: *Chelsea, The Hudson Review, The New Yorker, The Noble Savage, Poetry: A Magazine of Verse*, and *The Virginia Quarterly Review*.

# Contents

I

II

# III

# IV

V

# PART I

## Prologue to His Book

—To say
In words the way
The wave, the cloud—
To read aloud
The last wings in the late air,
Interpret the faint character
Of the still flower;
Tell
What mute leaves spell;
Pronounce the dew,
The hushed scent, the silent hue;
To speak, to say
With speech, This way,
See, See, It was this way
The hills, the wind—
To say, Grief was as if. . . .
To say, And love . . . love . . . To say,
Yes, Yes, It was like this,
This way—

## The Tale

The Enchanted Pilgrims said,
No, no, it is not far—
We were not long—The way
Lies past these clouds of light.
Though forged of quartz and iron
It is a little star.
Ice-crystal is its air.
We walked in winter there,
Bright snow fell on our capes.
In Spring we saw the small
Fruit forming on the boughs.
Always at evening
The carved coasts shone. The sky
Stained the great waves. Night
Moved slowly through those lands
With many lights. Always,
They told us, that world turned.
We thought at times a pure
Rain fell like light.
The wind was distant bells.
Forms resembling men
Walked in the valleys. Shapes
Like men moved in the hills.
Strange beasts dwelt there, they said.
We knew not if the leaves
Were true nor yet the stars.
They told us the faint hills,
The intense mountains, all,
—The waves, the glass of sky—
Were only coloured mists.
No man was certain these
Were not the fields of sleep.

We being bound believed. We
Trusted to the dreamt
Land. We drank of the
Dream waters. We pursued
Down immaterial
Autumn and ghostly spring
Time's wraith, the phantom year.
—O, *Earth* is exceeding fair:
Go, go, be happy there.

## Wishes for His Poem

Have at its source
No mood
But sorrow, not less perforce
To the heart than blood.

Evoke, to devise this thing,
Some influence fierce as waves',
As the rage of spring
Trembling with storms of leaves:

Such influences as define
The hue, the exact design
Of the rose
Even before its earliest leaves unclose.

May the infinite move within
The infinitesimal,
As in the particle
The atom's planets spin:

Integral and complete
As forests in a seed,
As the blue
Of all heaven in a prism of dew:

Bright, perfect, and austere
As the star-clear
Frost-flake
No storm may bend or break:

Stilled and significant at once
As
Amid ancient grass
Bones.

When it is wrought at last,
Though its seed were unrest,
Though very doom
The soil whence it must bloom,

Let it forget what grief
Gave it birth,
As from infernal earth
The innocent leaf—

Let it recall no more
Than flower or fruit
The darkness at its core,
The chaos at its root.

# Dirge

*Where is he now that shook to hear*
*The cuckoo cry, these many springs?*
Now shapes the wooden branch its bud.
The dull snake stirs in the dark hill.

*Where is he? Fares he well or ill?*
The spider spreads its glistening rings.
The gilded pheasant walks the wood.
The cuckoo's cry is hung on air.

# To Man

Protagoras 321

Of all things summoned forth
From mysterious earth,
Creation's brood, grotesque
As creatures in a masque—

The fish in the cold tall
Stream, the stag in brake,
The bear, the rippling snake
Escaping from its caul,

The sidling wolf, the bird
Swimming resistant wind,
And the blunt mole immured
Within twilight sand

—You only, kindless creature,
Seem fashioned as the least
Being in all nature,
Neither bird nor beast.

Creature without wings
Or fur or beetle's armor,
The mindless brutes go warmer,
And the creeping things.

The dreamless stone lasts longer
And cries not to be fed
But you shall find no bread
To assuage your hunger.

To assuage your thirst
You shall find no water;
The witless grass at worst
Fares a little better.

Yet come, and in a breath
Ascend to the mind's height;
Brood as an angel might
Upon the world beneath;

Think, all—the gigantic sphere,
Ice-capped, with quivering green
Oceans, whirled within
Its globe of cloud and air,

—Bird, beast, flower, and star
Are of no thing but thought,
Since if mind wills, they are,
Or if mind wills, are not.

The Rose surviving Time
Is patterned in your brain;
Without such paradigm
No rose had ever been.

Here, locked in the lean wire
Of your nerves, upstart
The waves, the rustling fire;
You bear within your heart

The lightning's silver blood;
The crystal blood of rains
You take into your veins,
And the wind's wild fluid;

Though you be less than strong
You bear the moons that climb;
Though you endure not long
No thing outlasts your time;

Though you be slight and small,
When your hour is flown
With your faint lamp you shall
Have taken the great sun.

Space never was so wide
As bursts the brain apart;
Time is the human heart
Set beating in the side.

Be comforted at length,
Be brave; till you be free,
Accept this frailty
That tenders you this strength.

## Essay on Deity

God's body is all space.
He is the shifting land
And the lifting seas.
He is the turning wind.
Like waters, all his strange
Substance suffers change
Forever, yet is known
Forever to be one.
Though water dress as blue
Wave or mist or dew
Or ice at the world's end,
It is one element.
Even as waters he
Takes shape of cloud and tree.
I see his essence plain
In transparent rain
And blowing mist: I know
His presence in the snow.

How then, embittered dust
But hostaged unto death,
Thought you to refuse
Your substance to his use?
To every glint of dust,
To every spark of frost,
To every grain of sand
He set his shining hand,
He breathed his shining breath.
How thought you to withstand,
Narrow heart, this power
That touches dimmest star,
That pierces finest seed?
Narrow brain, how thought

Your thinking to shut out
The undimensional Mind?
And you, most narrow sight,
You glass set in the skull,
Reflecting the least leaf,
The littlest flake to fall,
How thought you to lie blind
To that absolute light?

Yet since he everywhere,
In water, land, and air,
Move as everything—
The gull on stony wing,
The sliding rock, the fish
In the sea's dim mesh—
Then, minute breast of bone,
Behold how all unknown
You drew him home as breath
In crystal lapse and flood.
Heart that refuses God,
You bear him for your blood;
Obdurate mouth, he is
The food that fed your hunger.
Deny him then no longer;
You took him for your bread.
Behold how unaware
In breathing the wild air,
In seeing, being fed,
In knowing even now
These words, this mist and snow,
These birds at the earth's rim,
Whether you will or no,
You have accepted him.

## Madrigal

The heart grief took for instrument,
Once shaken by its own piteous sound,
Returns to be a heart no more:
Sooner may music return
From the wind to the strung wires;
Sooner the burnished wood inclined
To lute's shape or viol's
And bound with the thin strings,
May put forth leaves and be
Again an innocent tree.
Happier the nightingale,
Whose grief is music and no more,
Or water, whose sorrow is
Only its motion's sound,
Or air, or aught else music claims,
Than this hollow thing
Echoing if a hand
Touch it, or a wind.

# Arabesque

Love given from the sighing breast,
Once lost from the heart's core,
Is dark as the expense of blood
Till the heart beats no more.
And all its sorrow buys at last,
And would sell straightway, if it could,
Is but a simple thing,
A wisdom any child had guessed.
It is that love goes in the end.
It is that of all this amazement and pain,
The bright harm, the royal woe,
The brilliant wound and the stain,
Naught shall remain
To blazon one rose-leaf,
To illumine a prism of snow
Or a rainbow's crystal, to
Incline the course of wind
A gull's-wing's width, to bend
The worn sea to a wave:
It is that of all the full heart gave
Only the burden may remain.
This is all love gives,
This is all love can tell,
And the mind knows this well;
But the heart breaks if it believes.

## Spring Ghost

Just now, in snowy woods somewhere,
The first arbutus leaves break clear
Secretly, while yet the day
Lies an hour or so away,
And trees know. The barbed crystal star
Wanes westward, and at five there are
Lanterns borne slowly toward the shed
Amid the dark snows, and in bed
Wan sleepers sigh and turn: at six
A frosty light comes up and takes
The topmost vane above the barns,
And cattle stand with hay in horns
Beyond the luminous window-square
To watch the red round sun in air,
And harness reddens on the wall,
And rump by rump in the vague stall
Amid the glimmering straw the broad
Sleek stallion and his mare must stand,
And in the changing glow beyond,
The new colt, rusty-haired and rough,
Drinks burnished water from the trough,
And mice peep sharp-eyed out from straw.

By mid-morning the first thaw
Discovers leaves and fragile bones
Of field-mice, and bird-skeletons,
Draws from the charged earth the deep worm
That stony hail and winterstorm
Drove under; the prismatic air
Flows bright and chill as snow-water.
Blue as ice the puddles lie,
Reflecting cloud and branch and sky

And wings; and the slow spring at last
Builds up what autumn has laid waste.

And he that walks, arisen again,
Shall find the iridescent thin
Corselet of the serpent's skin,
Cast when the pulsing snake no more
That diamond armour could endure,
And the curious winding-cloth
Wherein the worm became the moth;
But not in the scarce-flowering brake
Fallen, nor drowned in the pure lake,
Nor crumpled amid winter grass,
The dead youth that he once was.

# Children

They are mysterious and proud. They have secrets from us.
  They remember perhaps what we no longer may.
  They see with grave eyes through the shapes of our world
  As if through the pure shapes of ice or quartz,

Inferring there is something we do not understand
  Beyond what we know, the firm lands, the stone mountains,
  —As if we were children reading, spelling out
  The patterned letters, not the meaning word.

The same doors open to us, but they lead us elsewhere,
  And the same windows but we turn and the scene changes:
  We do not see the fantastic birds nor the striped rain,
  We do not walk in a wood that fades if we waken.

They learn how the butterfly wakes, how the pale pear
  Takes colour, how through the summer nights the stems slowly
      without sound
  Rise, and the blossoms explode, noiseless,
  The pods burst scattering silk and the sear stalks tremble;

They are taught how the spider sinks in the soft log,
  Abandoning his rayed rings, how the autumn fly
  Hangs withering in the strung web, and the midge beside him,
  Mute, and the aged leaves converse in the night arbour.

—All their passion is a passion of weeping.
  They are innocent of woe. They think it a scratched knee.
  They never heard of the love that breaks us.
  The loss they know is of a coin or a topstring.

They pretend, knowing there is nothing but the semblance.
  They examine indifferently the dead, or simulate sorrow.

They do not meet themselves upon the stair.
They never confront the unknown face in the mirror.

They see how at dusk the snow falls, illumining softly
    Wherever it falls, and the faces strange in the upward shine,
    They go out at last as into cold moon-country.
    They shout in the lunar forests and a cry confirms them.

They dream of journeys. They do not know of a journey
    Of men minute on a huge rocket of stone.
    Or perhaps they do. It is not known. They are reticent.
    They are simple and wise. They are wary. They are mysterious
        and proud.

## Catechism at Midnight

Frost-creak. Pale panes in the dark wall.
The ringed flame flags, prolongs, aspires,
Trembles. The first bell of twelve
Stays the mouse working in the wall.

Now wake. Arise. By candlebeam
Behold. The senseless animal,
Dumb monster driven by the mind,
Goes slack within its chair. Sighs. Sleeps.

Veiled spirit risen like thin breath
To brood above the unconscious clay,
Not crust nor cup hath fed thee here.
—Nay, nor crumb bird-beak let fall.

Thou whom no craft of clasp or key
Constrains, nor clock nor calendar,
Say what enchantment binds thee.—Hush.
I stay: yet vanish, if I will.

—Angel of the wind wert thou,
Cold cloud thy dwelling.—Peace. Peace.
Translucent image, the wind too
Wears dust, yet lays it down at will.

—Outside the sparklet forms, falls.
Now bell-sound wanes from the late bell.
The sighing flame breaks clear. Thou too,
Thou too go forth, be free— —Nay, nay,

Nay, homeless else, I tarry here.

# Colloquy

When shall this weight be cast
That droops the spirit's spray?
*With birds it will lift at last.*
*With the leaves it will blow away.*

How shall the spirit be
When this thing is done?
*As a bough, and the birds flown.*
*As a leafless tree.*

# Novel in Pictures

## I

He is a child.
          He lives
In an ancient house
Known to the wind. Believes
Images of boughs
Cast on the rainy window
Are giants reaching into
The nursery.
          Recalls
Slow lights along the halls
At dusk. Remembers there
Gleams upon a chair,
Stair-creak,
          a sigh,
                    the wind
With night rain,
          and last
A woman on a stair,
Mysterious, looking down,
Silent, in her hand
A taper, the thin flame
Leaf-shaped. The other hand
Clutches at her breast.

Nothing more.
          Unknown
She comes at night to stand
In the wild mind, her eyes
Immense and dark, as one
At the sill of night. . . .

## II

It is past midnight.
                Rain,
Impromptu, soft as air,
Moves in boughs and eaves
With a sound like bells and strings.
Afterwards the drain
Drips,
        as straightening leaves
Spring back;
              as each austere
Small quicksilver sphere
Prolongs and falls;
              as wake
In cold leaf-light the young
Birds, sharp-eyed, and shake
Diamond wings.
             The pane
Clears, projecting now
The faint print of a bough
With leaves across the bed.

## III

He comes in sleep upon
A stream where a broad swan
Steers her slow ship, her
Long throat arched, her eyes
Secret, her blown plumage
Crystal-shafted
             And
He stretches forth his hand
To the immaculate bird

With her glimmering image
Drifting,
       but the swan
Sees not:
       She drifts on.

## IV

He has been ill.
       He stands
In the dusk, his hands
Frail, his fingers clutching
The cold sill.
       Stands watching
Through print branches where
The mysterious lamplighter
Stands in snow—his breath
Issuing like his ghost
Into darkening air—
And lifts flame lampward with
His staff to the tall post
And cage of glass:
       whereto
At once must waft and blow
And float on filmy wing
Round the pinned fluttering
Flame,
       the moths of snow.

## V

Bronze and iron and glass,
The carved Americas
Lie clasped in the glazed coils
Of cold sliding streams.

Waves lift. The waters roar
Like wind, from the seawall
To sea to green seafloor
Raging like wind:
                              In gloom
Niagara plunges home;
East, the sea unrolls
Against the Atlantic shore;
Off Newfoundland the veiled
Wind fluent amid rocks;
Off Scotland the curved waves
Plough the seas' land.
                              Mist
Flies over England.
                              Rain
In bronze fields to the west.
North, the timeless snow
Sifts through the great
Hourglass of the air.
South, the shapeless wind
Walks in the wet night. . . .

And seas,
                    and presently
Land,
          and presently—

The boy by firelight
Reads geography.

## VI

In stormy fall of light
He stands where waves come in

At the lake-front.
                    White
Lofty lightning blows
Its brief leafless boughs
Till the air like a great bell
That hung tongueless and still
Tolls,
          and through beating air
Falls,
          like sudden hush
Over leaf and bush,
The soft sound of rain.

## VII

Light breaks on her face,
Her eyes are shut. Her mouth
Is like a leaf. Her hair
Is like gold leaves. Her bare
Frosty shoulder gleams
With cold light.
                    Her breath
Makes mist.
                    The lamp flames
And fails. . . .

## VIII

He stands at the moving rail.
His coat flaps. His trousers flutter.
Far down the glass of sea
Heaves. The reflected sky
Runs along icy decks.
Above, the extended gulls
Revolve. The salt snow falls.

Beyond, in dusky fog,
Pinnacle, bell-tower,
Steeple, castled wall,
Precipitous,
                    the glowing glass
Bergs loom like a strange tall
Town.
            The letter blows
At last from the gloved hand,
Seaward. He does not move. He
Stares down at the white water.

His coat flaps. His trousers flutter.

## IX

Negro in dumb-show, now,
Weightless, his shadow glides
Before him over brilliant
Snow and branch-shadows.

Tall blackamoor, strange friend,
Dark self, infernal brother,
Dream, daemon, shape of night—

Or is this then that Other
Masked and cowled in shade
That confronts him here. . . .

O mute Companion!

## X

The bright voluminous steam
Ascends through iron beams

To the dim dome.
                    The long
Train, its windows glowing,
Waits on the dark track.
Motionless he stands
In darkness of the piled
Baggage.
          A bell is beating—

## XI

          She stands
Upon the stair.
                    His hands
Tremble lifting the flame
To his lips. His gaze
Reflects the flame.
                    He says
Slow words.
          The slow
Clock ticks.
          The flames play,
The snow falls.
                    She turns away.

## XII

Walks late at night, the street
Resonant. Leaves fall
Through dismantled boughs.
His breath smokes. At his feet
Scurry the brown leaves
Like rats in cellar and hall.

This is the vacant house
Of autumn, halls of wind,
Structure of leaves, the eaves
Straining, the broken shutter
Beating, the porch swept bare,
The swarms of leaves at the gutter:

Ghost with hat and stick,
You late wanderer,
Your bright breath wastes in air:
Rage fails in your breast:
Even grief dies at last
And is buried here.

Love only will not rest.

# PART II

## Liber de Causis

The Babylonian said,
In shape of thunder and storm
Marduk slew Tiamat,
And of that trunk enorm
Star, sea, and beast were made;
Lastly, a certain clay.
There seems no doubt of that.

No, No, another cried,
The Earth is but a ball
The Dung-beetle rolls round
To hatch out his own will.
If smaller creatures still
Elect to walk that sphere,
That is their own affair.

But up the west came the wild day,
Twelve stars and a red cindrous sun,
And fast in that prodigious dawn
The scroll of reason burnt away;
And air grew dark and wild,
And something monstrous walked
Like earthquake, and towns rocked,

And sky cracked burning at both ends,
And there an idiot Giant rose
And with huge hairy hands
Seized the Thunder-Tree
And shook down worlds like fruits
And plucked up the Universe by the roots;
Nor deigned to notice me.

# Anthropos

First in a wilderness of fern and steam
The Soul moved fearfully in the new guise:
The monstrous man-shape; tusked, shaggy, still with the ape-stoop;
Shambling with swung knuckles; stub-tailed; unclean;
Fitted with eyes that glittered in his face;
Sleeping in sea-rock, in the cave cut by the sea-whorl;
In pits in the earth; in the high tree-branches;
Eating the thigh of the deer while the flesh still trembled;
Peering with red eyes where the strange she squatted,
Her excrement smoking in the savage grass;
Having such speech as beasts have; amazed with fright,
Falling upon his face at tremendous dawn;
Hiding his young from starlight; from the huge moon
Crawling in terror; fearing echoes and reflections;
Suspicious of bird-calls, wary of the rock's shadow;
Seeing death in all shapes and fighting it;
Battling the grasping hawk; strangling the finned snake;
Grappling with harpies, flinging stones at the thunder;
And in the end being always overcome,
Drawing up his legs and stretching them; so perishing;
Unless the beast pinned him with a paw and
Fed of the quivering belly as the dying eyes watched,
While the young, defiant, shrieking, their hair standing,
Spat from the pinnacle on the feeding beast;
—Leaving for signature the arch of a rib or a smashed skull,
And a cave scratched with a bear's shape, and one or two stones.

## Abailard Sleeps at His Book

What time the body drowsed in chair,
Mouse fed in platter, and flame wagged;
Cup glimmered in cupboard; the cold stair
Creaked; the house stiffened; the wind flagged.

As lax flesh, mindless, and unstrung
To purpose, slept like any beast,
Moon stood at window and stared long;
Spectral the lit branch; snow fell, ceased.

Spire and hutch with lucent snow
Sparkled minutely; all shone, shone
As if the earth had been the moon,
Till all waned with the waning glow.

Then in the waste night flame on wick
Perished; the lean worm unseen
Consumed the subtlety of the Greek;
Rime thickened on hinge and pane.

Lastly, amid dark snows a bird
Chirped; the house grew colder still;
And the mute animal sighed, stirred,
Restive to the returning will.

# The Night Journey

I went in woldway dark as sleep,
Bearing no lantern save the mind's.
I mournfulness had for cloak and hood.

Thence morningward through the sad veils
Rode I, nor knew what mount I rode,
But came on castled ruin at last,

And beat on the great graven bell.
That weft-world lifted then as lifting
Mist-fold: mead, stream, draped barge drifting

Saw I, and Three cypress-stoled,
That shewed One bound and burning-haired,
Whose only substance was sky-gold,

And Him they wounded in the side,
And named the eternal wound as Time,
And never might its loss be stayed;

Though naught but roses did He bleed,
Nathless the holy sufferer died,
And all His body was Day-spring;

And me they changed into a bird,
And to a ferny bough I flew,
And of Sir Gawaine and the Sword

And of the Christ-Cup did I sing.

# The Assumption

Joy to the Spirit came:
Souls, or stars, in air
Gleamed like a host of flowers.
Quietness they wore,
As lilies laden with dew.
Still Eternity
Lay on them like sleep.
For in heaven's shadowless halls,
Since all Time's measure ran,
Naught stirred; the cloud-hung slow
Clocks with weight and wheel
Moved never, nor Hourglass
Let fall one burnished sand.
Motionless there the deep
Wind, and the pure bell
Struck when One was born
Rang still, and gave forth
Not sound but beating light.
Fingers invisible touched
Harps, but the glistening strings
Wrought perfume, and not sound.
And bright-harnessed, fire-haired,
As silent, tall, as bright
As holy candles are,
Angels waited in
Perpetual Sabbath sheen. . . .

*O fields almost earth-fair!*

# The Crusade

You might have said it was a fine thing, save for the poor folk.
We had heard of it, we had thought it would be a magnificence
Of kings, dukes, knights, and barons, a heartening, a bright
Motion of metal horses and metal men,
The wind battling with banners, and all that.
Some of us could not sleep for news of their coming.
We stood on the dark mountain listening among many leaves
And strove to see what so many hermits had talked of,
Angry with the late crickets and the waterfall for their noises;
And when the air glimmered at last, we saw them
Under the high hawks turning above the valley.
Ahi! We saw quite enough of them in their marching;
Our thatch and our doorstones stank of them seven days:
Dull faces and fierce eyes, but fierce for food,
Or sleep, or something other than what was spoken of,
And, for the most part, poor folk looking frightened
And, it may be, ashamed; fluttering with rags and tatters as the autumn with leaves;
And endless carts and baggage, and sick horses.
They had got tired of carrying the heavy banners,
Had laid them in the wagons; as for the fiery mail,
What we saw was rusty; the rest must have jostled the pots and pans.
We were puzzled to know which were the noble lords.
Later we heard they had taken Jerusalem:
I thought of a wandering like an eviction of the poor,
Like villagers fleeing a fire or a plague,
And I thought too what their guides were: a goose and a goat.

It comes upon me, men are most strange creatures.
No doubt we have fine thoughts at certain times;

But most things we do seem to end in folly and misery.
Since that sight I have thought much of Paradise:
If it should be less than's promised, or not be at all,
It would be hard to know what to say to the poor folk.

# G. M. H. Asks the Question in the Fells

March 17, 1889

What am I but a base mechanic thing—
Time's engine, it may be—; hours, minutes I mark
And not spend; all my lust, joy, shame but being
A dial's signs, to eke out bright and dark.
I, Sire, do mark what kills me; but live not;
Get not; wreak not; signify the times done,
Hours, years lost, without memory, that but got
More times unmeaning; mark men's hour, and mine own;
All the heart's motion counting oblivion.

Or, Sire, I do, mortally, as a man stabbed,
Bleed inwardly; have so much life, at most,
As may suffice Death; lose that, O, like blood;
Have not blood, even—no—to show how much hath ebbed.
And here even stone blooms; the morning mountains brood
Great with much green; lambed sheep graze; the goosemaid
Goes with the gay flock; lark sings above meadowplaid;
All's lovely with suit of thy service; hath sheen of the Host;
All's lit, thy candles: field, flower, and tree.
I alone serve not; serve nothing; myself, nor Thee.

## The Atonement

The martyr amid golden fires
Cried out: "While Red Knight fought with Black,
The White Lady, with both their squires,
Made the beast with double back;

And while the great St. Austin preached,
So air grew gold with angels' wings,
A beggar scratched because he itched;
I perish to amend these things,

And while in blazing shirt I stand,
Priest jostles knave in the dark street,
Better to see my burning hand
Fall off, and sputter at my feet."

# Byzantium

He whom the cord, the smoking dart
Once so troubled that he died,
As elder mysteries foretold
Has risen from his shroud in pride,
And burns in fires of burning gold.
And though no sanctity has healed
The wounds that broke his limbs apart,
A splendour rings the suffering head,
Cleft flesh is crystal now, the heart
Where more than mortal anguish dwelt
Is but a jewel in the side,
And its spent flames but rubies spilled,
Like angels' blood, and jewel-cold.

# Sonnet

I have served Thee; give me mine hire, O Lord.
Thy seed I planted; Thine the grain to be:
Behold the hollow husk, the blackened gourd;
Fools, affluent, mock; Thy Self goes mocked in me.

Why gavest Thou me this bitter grace, to sow,
No fruits intended? No especial thing,
As grain cloud-grown; recalled frost; virtuous snow;
Or winter warmed, I ask; but spring in spring,

Winter in wintry season.—Invisible
Turner of seasons! Artificer of storms! Thou! Hear, O, behold:
Pied fields lift flourishing; lambs leap; orchards, alight, shine
Aloft with leaved fruit, in the lands not thine;
Thy boughs stand birdless on the summer hill;
Thy lambs lie stiffening in the summer fold.

## Imago Mortis

After the long siege in the waterless valley
Of stones scattered like skulls,
After the great collision in the winter pass
Of armoured horses and banners and armoured men,
I returned to my palace; there wedded; at the wedding banquet,
Touched the gift of Luigi, my brother, the Pious.
Then it was, as one fallen in full armour,
My soul strove to move my corpse, and could not.
In consequence of my rank I was interred,
Not with the common bone-chalk and grave-powder,
But here, pinned down by a magnificent statue
Of myself as I shewed in armour and on horseback.
And in the twelfth midnight past my change,
Three of my nephews, thinking of these jewels,
Visited me, with crowbars and with lanterns;
Looked in, grinning with anguish; stared upon
The subtil fiction of my flesh almost
Dissolved; the spotted face half-eaten,
Teeming; the raw spine wreathed with serpents;
Beard, hair yet growing, flourishing in my destruction,
The nails also; the jewelled poisonous man
Passive in's rich shroud, big with worse corruption;
Thereafter in my peace I learned what death is.

Ay but death is a terrible and proud thing!
When the Fleshmonger had seized on his last fee,
When the soul had risen from the terraced Mountain,
The self remained, that was neither flesh nor soul;
Remained and listened; slept not; listened, heard
Five hundred years pass; heard the walled steep town
Thrice burn; heard, and listened still, and heard
Siege of autumnal storms, wheels, whispers, leaves, footfalls;

And rumour of much war; as cannon, pestilence, and weeping;
And listened yet a thousand years and heard
The bells swinging and striking in the wind,
The night-shrouds settling, far down at the town's base;
Lastly, goats, or deer, running on scattered stones; but heard no
   more
Of man-sound ever; yet listened and yet listens.

Mage,
Thing of what world I know not, but not of this,
Think that the listening and intelligent dead
Know of the waste world; think that in death
So horrible and so powerful grows the will,
So they but willed so, the unstarved shrewd bones
Might stand and seize the ways and the still towns,
Might war, wed, take crown and vesture, traffick in much greed—ay,
Out of the infinite wisdom of the will
Might send their monuments moving through the streets—
But of their wisdom do not; but lie still,
Unto eternity making with these bones
The sign and emblem of the Emperor.

## "Socrates mused a day and night"

Socrates mused a day and night
And from a clearer wisdom cried:
*Perseus upon counting-stool,*
*The noble heart beats all unguessed;*
*Andromeda weds knave or fool;*
*Another slays the wave-borne beast.*

# Gian Maria concerning Death

My nativity said, I should die of a shaft and a stone.
When the great stone struck me, hurled from the castled wall,
When the arrow entered to the shuddering groin,
I that had fought in armour for five days
Fell with that armour; fell headlong like an image of iron;
Briefly then in the hollow helm the jaws ground; the mailed hands
Clenched and unclenched, plucking up weeds and grasses;
Agony of the animal only; the man was dead;
And for a long time afterward blood came through the chains.
When a year had passed without word from any of us,
My father paused before Vittoria's chamber,
Ordered the Latin, the candles, the steeples tolling,
Cypress to be worn a whole year on each hutch and kennel of the
    town.
Meanwhile here at Ravenna the crows struck at the steel,
And in the armour lay the rotted man.

Ai but death is a piteous profound thing!
Live men know but the name's sound and a fear;
Children bandy with that most simple word.
I Gian Maria, son of the Duke Francesco,
Having no monument but the beautiful armour of Mirandola,
Forgot the confusion of standards and metal men;
Learned, O, what death is: ai misery of the unburied!
Ai how the flesh runs seething; feel of the moon's cold
And naked starlight on the naked spine;
And how through that long anguish the sick soul
Broods like a dog grieving by a grave.

Thou summoner and questioner of the dead,
Thou canst not guess on that great majesty;
Yet when armour and cloth and the last rag and shred

Of the beast are torn from thy perduring bones,
Thou shalt not ask but answer; thou shalt behold
In the black sleep of that gigantic night
What image the ephemeral flesh hath hid from thee.
Thou shalt know, seeing thine everlasting bones,
Thou art Death's self; thou art person'd Death; thou shalt die
And thy death close thee as a sepulchre,
Mute, motionless, perpetual, though vast wind
Winnow the atoms of the universe,
Altering the ancient order and design;
And centuries shall be but phases of thy sleep,
And history, the mixed imagery of thy dream.

# Winter Marketplace

December dusk like fog withdraws
The form but leaves the substance still.
Mute emanation from dim drains
And street-stones desolate and chill,
The night comes, a gloom rising there
Amid the wheels of wagons, as
Stairs sink: as doorways fade
Dumbly: as the hucksters' nags
Stand motionless in mounting shade.
Hueless, the awning hangs in dusk.
The last roofstone burns and wanes.

Now circled lamps alone recall,
Vaguely, as memory to the mind,
The wraiths once thought substantial
Before sense faltered and went blind;
And sunk like things in a time done
Or forms beheld in sleep, faint house
On house confronts the shuttered square,
And pavement, rail, and standing wall
Leap, soundless, if a lamp-flame's blown,
Or vanish if that sleeper rouse
Who stands unseen, anonymous there.

He sees through shifting glooms. He sees
The wares in cart and lanterned stall,
The sidewalks crowded with cooped fowl,
With baskets, with felled winter trees:
Sees, past the cold misty panes,
The meats, the glowing fruits piled high,
The glazed cakes. As in fear he turns
To the strange faces glimmering by,

And suddenly, seeing, himself is drawn,
Webbed in the deep dream. He walks on,
He is caught in the dark crowds. He is gone.

Caught amid moving shapes of men,
He must walk with the many feet
Following in the invisible maze,
Nor may his footsteps' sound again
Be ravelled from those devious ways,
But now obscurity and chill
Move everywhere with the loose wind,
The lamps plunge, the blind papers blow,
And if in like unrest or no
With him, or in some kinder wind,
The sign swings all night without end.

## Voice Heard from the Third Planet

Artificer, within whose perilous brain
The starlight leaf and the far boughs of air
Alike were wrought, and moons, and diminutive man
Bound to a grassy sphere,

Lean from the cloud-high leaf, the unwithering
Branch, the celestial Tree of Moons, to him
Caught in the dreams of winter and of spring:
Descend, Daemons and fiery Seraphim,

Take pity on this talking animal:
Possessed by angels and impelled by fiends,
He turns, enchanted, with the turning ball,
The turning sky, the winds.

O change his body to a marble hind,
Take back his spirit to the phantasmal Grove,
Into a tiger's form translate his mind,
And make his heart a dove.

# The Discourse on the Usual Matter

Salvation, said Satan,
Cannot be dissociate from perdition.
Thus the white stag, that drank of the white well,
Standing white in the white moon,
Yet shapes a delicate stag of shade.
Or say, a swan drifts on its image:
So in the clear soul is the pure ill
Wrought of very purity; perfect as it.

—The anguish that I have at heart,
If indeed that sorrow be the soul,
Made answer for me: All night the deformed dream
Lay upon me; I watched by the drowsed monster
As to preserve the dead from demons.
At seven it woke, beheld the lights of rain,
Dressed, with clouds descending to the streets,
As carts creaked by with yellow fog between the wheels.
And while the street lamps burned by day,
The beast fed of its dish, its cup.
Now this greater horror is loosed upon me:
It muses, and by some miracle of mind the air
Speaks, the air speaks, in an empty room.

Appearance and reality, said Satan,
Are one, or if not one, seem one, in that both are seeming.
Fog makes the city gloomy as an old museum:
Go, visit the horrible raree-show;
Remark the waxworks walking in the streets,
Take in the odd sights: next door, while you slept,
I have entreated one to a charming murder
—Observe the curious staring at the doors.
And in that house narrow and straight, like a coffin set on end,

Or Caligari's cabinet, what of morning?
Shame requires only the drawn blinds.
There male and female take their carnal postures;
It is not too late to see the timid man
Effect his violence upon paid girls.
Or take my monocle—see hell-fire in all windows.
Shall we view the bottled mermaid?
Shall we stop and see the lady sawed in half?

The anguish in me cried out like a child frightened at the theater,
This is the abyss, this is the very crater,
And the beast I govern stands like a beast, beholding.
What is it human creature can behold,
Beholding the sad carnival? What can it see
Unguessed of gods, what privy vision of devils?

Shall we pause, said Satan, shall we talk of Good and Ill?
How pleasant is error to the erring mind!
It is cousin to this unsubstantial substance
Diffusing between the townsfolk and the town,
Cloud coloured like the crêpe at doors where aged women have died.
Distinguish, now, the murderer and the saint.

But the personage who figures in all histories
Hearing again the discourse of the Irrefragable Doctor
And the Doctor Seraphic, on the usual matter,
With hat and stick descended to the streets,
Passing the Judgment Angel on the stair;
And bought a damp newspaper, waited for a cab.

# The Christmas Meditation

This is the dead center of the year,
The day's and the year's midnight, and the soul's.
From winter steeples standing in the moon
Great bells are telling the ancient names of Time,
And every bell that in dark belfry tolls
Beats as much on the mind as on the ear,
Not recounting that old marvellous tale,
But crying of some greatness to be born.

What can be born so great as the old loss?
I count up only one year's dead:
I shut the book and face the casement squares,
Facing the moon, the steeples, the dull snows,
And face reality: nothing that can be,
Neither an actual nor a fabled thing,
However holy, however beautiful,
Need think to stand one moment in their stead.

How should a Form suffice the mortal sin?
Was all that suffering wrought upon a dream
That bled fantastically from its ghostly wounds,
Or was it indeed the informed actual god
Perished, twisting and crying upon a cross
Whereof the huge shade chilled the Roman kings?
Neither a god's death could suffice that loss,
Nor birth of any greatness yet unborn.

I wavering between belief and unbelief
Speak out: I too, as any human thing,
Stare for one instant on the fateful cup,
Certain at last of that most suspect grief,
That one's but human, whatever be divine,

And for the sake of some half-legendary thing
Put fear aside, accept, drink the last drop
Of the whole vessel of human suffering.

I say the beggar's step amid wan snows,
The babe's late cry, the dog's midnight howl,
The wars, the truces, the whole human tale,
Whether trivial or great, is purposeless,
Save, in some wild fashion, all sufficed,
As fall of minute sands within a glass
Accomplishing the mystery of an Hour,
To bring about the strange cyclical birth of Christ.

And what if somewhere now in an ancient town,
As all this ringing metal prophesies,
There be enacted that most ancient play
Of a god's agony in a human guise?
It matters nothing; gods in changeless skies
Serve but to regulate the night and day,
And the stars' circlings; it is man's blood alone
Suffices both to err and to atone.

## The Angel of the Annunciation

Mortal hand, O exquisite,
Here in the holy book of Spring,
With gold fallen from a star,
Gild now an angel's wing.
Bend now one keen luminous line
To circle a celestial brow.
Turn, alter, trace no more
The mortal heart's design.
Depict the angled sword,
The burning hair, the calm
Feet that tread the abyss of storm,
The archèd wings so wide
Noon's glow and star-sheen fall on either side;
The substance, O, star-clear,
Being indeed but air.
O hide all in consuming cloud,
In dews of saints', of martyrs' blood,
And if the unquiet heart must blazon still
The anguish of its veins,
Take the fierce colour it contains.

## Late Encounter

What art Thou?—Speak.
*One whose name the wind*
*Strives to shape, and the pure bell*
*And the wave and the trancèd stone would tell.*

Mine is Thy Form. Thy Face,
White, white in the mist,
Master, is mine.
*Ay, thine.*
*Yet, beneath all faces, mine.*

Bleak is this coast: the hooded wave
Walks at the land's edge.
The wind walks in the sedge.
*This is the Earth's end.*

*Yet lies remoter land.*
*Mist is in that place.*
*Birds call from the high wind.*
—Not to that bourne I fare.

*A bright land lies beyond.*
*They have joy, dwell there.*
Nay, nay,
I stay.

*Last land of all is Nought—*
*Not the shape of the wind in the dead grass,*
*Not the storm shaped to the wind's hollow.*
—Still would I stay.—*Alas,*
*Still must thou follow.*

# The Devil in Crystal

Set here a waste scene; sea, sky like funeral sables;
By black sea a harsh hill; a tower set thereon
With one light burning; now let there be storm,
Thunder, shaken lightning, lurid rain,
And seven demons sailing on green cloud,
And let the Time, in black hat and black cloak,
Creep like a murderer upon the Place.
Summon the pale spectators.—The Play begins.

"Look!" says the Doctor, in the tower room.
"I have set all in order—flame sings, clear glass glows,
Crucible bubbles, brightens; now you shall see."
The dog with cat's head grafted slinks from the chamber.
Around, in wire cages feathered mice
Turn flame-lit eyes; clock ticks like bomb,
Marking the Time.
                    *"I behold, Master, a sphere*
*Turning in cloud and storm; thereon are laid*
*Waters, and lands; the lands quake, the seas rage.*
*I behold a wilderness, a black hill, a black tower:*
*Within are two men and a candle-flame."*

The Doctor laughs; strokes sharp beard. "Now I mix,
Now I decant; now add this blazing element,
Green seawater, blue aether; now examine."
Without the room howls catlike, now, the dog.
Lightning at window jigs like a bright forked man.

"A globe! White-hot; suspended; nothing upholds it!
I see lands and waters—I see towns and people upon it!"

"Precisely—precisely. But with this perfection:
The whole is evil; the pure absolute ill

Like a fatal jewel; like the devil in crystal.
O excellent formula!
                    "*Master, the thing is known,*
*The riddle unriddled; let the Trumpeter be summoned.*"

Let fall the curtain; so; the scene's at end.

## Cry before Birth

Babe cried within the womb,
Before oblivion fall
Upon the Soul and its doom,
I would speak of the Soul
And say, it hath seven rings
Burning with seven hues,
Image of those seven
Circles wrought in heaven
For the stars' wanderings.
Hence only what undoes
That wheel of the universe,
Of world and circling world,
May destroy the Soul.
Hence, what would this disperse,
First must shatter all.
I name it imperishable
And perfect beyond ill,
Since of its whirling rings
Every mote and beam
Is brilliant with God's fire;
And all the Soul's desire
To make perfect what it is
Is but a rose
In anguish to be a bird,
Of its own loneliness;
For all is as heaven's Lord
Ordains, wills, and allows.
And what if the Soul do ill?
So it keep innocence
To err of its own will,
Such is the virtue of that spirit

Evil itself turns excellence
If but Soul weave it, and Soul wear it,
Even that the Soul could be
Redeems all the Soul's worst:
Though Christ's cross was the curst
Wood of Adam's tree,
Judas died as well
Upon a bitter place,
Nor was that worse disgrace
Less acceptable.
I say there is naught but Soul;
Or, were all beside
Canceled and destroyed,
This in itself were all:
Tree, beast, flower, and star;
Ay; and more; and more.

## The Cock of Heaven

The glittering Cock of Heaven crew;
That cry turned wild gold and was Day.
Joy is not in Heaven, he saith,
But there the saints with sleeves of gold
(Each hath a moon attends his head)
Bend weeping to the misty storm,
And weep, and the fierce Seraphim
(Each hath a sun for gilded rim),
Cross-winged, bear the angled sky,
Weeping, and in rose-rain-light
Fallen from the glowing wounds of Christ
The mute sweet-wounded martyrs weep,
And winged Shapes walk the shafted wind.
—All weeping and all bright, bright,
For all who stand in Heaven's air
Are ringed like stars with a still sheen,
Gold-circled like the circled dews.
Though for Time's dark their weeping is,
They do but weep one night till dawn,
Till I crow heaven and earth away:
And at this hour I tell the Day.

## No. 10 Blucher Street

As fog—exhaled at ten from chimneys,
From pavements, drains, from watchmen's pipes,
From nostrils of tired cab-horses—

Ringed the street-lamp, withdrew the stair,
Dimmed the numeral on the door,
Wreathed the gold-gowned Seraphim

Leant past wires and clotheslines there;
As, beneath wet wooden gables,
Past drawn shades, the blue fly buzzed

Slowly above the still child; as
Magnified, the shadow moved
Weightless on wall-paper; as coiled springs

Squeaked to the skinny boy in spasm
Above a bought thing; as a hand
Soundlessly raised the sash; as in

Darkness the bald widower breathed
Darkness, his head within the oven;
As the tap dripped; as the cook, night-gowned,

Hair in curl-papers, yawned, wound
The belled clock; as the caged bird slept;
As the lamp smoked; as the landlady's cat

Stared at the motionless cockroach; as
Ahasuerus in skull-cap,
His beard glittering with drops of fog,

Turned key in lock and entered to
The flame burning in the misty hall—
—Gabriel, the Cock of Heaven, crew.

# The Wood of Vampires

"Me thou seest hanging in this blood-lit Wood,
  The dead heart beating yet, the blind eyes pulsing,
  A shape, web-winged, slavers, fastening on my genitals.

"I was of Rome, I seemed as the helmed Caesars.
  In the ruins are many coins stamped in my image.
  Statues of me still pose to the empty towns.

"I saw the millions battling with engine and cannon.
  Now unknown monsters breed on the heaped brick.
  Nowhere, now, in the Earth-light moves a man.

"Behold this horror that compels my ecstasy.
  Thou art accurst if thou pity me: I am a vile thing:
  I was of those who wrought the terrible war."

—"Image of Judas hanged I make of my death-form.
  Famous I was, among the perished nations.
  Nathless my name I speak not; thou wouldst but curse me.

"If thou wouldst learn it, demand of Germany
  What creature had of her such sufferance
  As now of me hath this winged clinging thing."

—"I was of Russia."—"Spain."—"I, like a cholera,
  Increased by corpses."—"Millions with engine and cannon."
  —"The dead heart beating."—"Nowhere."—"Demand of Germany."

—"Of Spain."—"Of Russia."—"Rome."—"Perished nations."

## Prometheus Speaks

I nailed on rock upon the eagle-wall
(Twelve million years amid the crashing cloud;
The bird beats, fastened with beak and claw upon me)

Behold the glass world; therein seven images
Formed of clear light move with seeming motion,
And seven of darkness wholly; all are mine.

Seven and seven illusions of contrary colour,
Moving in crystal, of one nailed motionless;
And the motion of these, the world's whole myth and history.

Thou that madest the Single and the Many
Thou hast made the One soul manifold with infinite mirrors;
It was myself beseiged myself at Troy;

Myself that slew myself in the beaked galleys;
Perseus and Andromeda and the Beast were I;
The betrayer and betrayed were always one,

Though the tale speak of many lands and kings.

# PART III

PART III

## Last Autumnal

Wild swans have cried out, with the cry
Of women in a tragedy
At the fall of a great house.
All's silent now, and yet
All's ended: the fountain blows,
The burning cloud rains down
Its golden influence still,
But the earth in calmness waits,
Like some doomed famous queen,
The darkening final scene.

Ten years earlier I
Might have made this the theme
Of autumnal melancholy,
And rounded it to a rhyme;
For my kind were always quick,
Before woe struck so deep,
To make much of seasons—could weep
Or laugh by the calendar,
As if all man's fortunes were
Weathers of earth and sky.

Now I stand and watch
Indifferently as the earth
Plays out her ancient play,
Unclasps her leaves and her roses,
In a feignèd death.
What matter these mummeries?
It is man who dies; it is
For him that the wind comes;
On him that the darkness closes.

# The Rebellion

Being sick of eternal and artificial autumn,
The fake trees with their torn autumnal hangings,
Sick of drinking out of the cracked inherited cups,
Why should I sit slippered, a young head beneath the inherited
    gray wig,
Here amid the wrecks of our old estate,
Why should I sit like all the other young men
Shut up each in his separate castle with the common ghost,
The old castles of our generation with one old crow circling all,
Crying out the old dismal prophecy;
What if one era and its history
Transformed to a rotten tapestry on a wall?
I, living solely to provide the stale dubious tragedy
Of the old fierce house dying out with the weak princeling dying,
What should I do but trouble a little the worm, the mouse,
Not arrest them, not preserve these fading cloths.

No, no, I smell the new wind, Danger: the cold new weather;
Pluck back this curtain, push the windows wide,
Here's clean snow on the sill, and look, look, stars—
The whole sky's full of lanterns still; why, there
The Pole Star glitters, aloft for mariners, there
The hunter's lit star, good emblems all, still true,
And all that stillness as if the earth stopt turning
Only the strict frost, moon's reflection in cold snows,
Where, at least, real wolves run, their teeth true pain.

I will quiz no dead kings more on the haunted platform,
No, not my father's armed shape; talk with no more devils or angels,
Not ride in rotten armor upon the old starved horse
To add more panels to the tedious allegory.
I will pull on boots, cut a stick, whistle a dog to heel,
And walk like a black fly up the fresh page of snow

Clear to the Northern Pole its starry rings,
And, it may be, make new civilization there,
Not in the old image of our pride, fake cities with all windows glowing
Like the candy villages under the Christmas tree,
Nor yet the ultimate and incredible hoped city,
But something like the huntsman's shelter, bound boughs of tamarack
    and fir,
Rude, made but in passing, yet suitable for a winter's night
    at least.

# Ice-Age

Winter fell on Europe. The snow sifted,
Gradual infiltration, incessant whisperings, flakes circulating
    innumerable as rumors and lies,
Masking cities, falsifying all shapes, freezing
Fear to a false calm, constricting
The continent under a heavy peace like ice.
Treacherous immobility of the frozen volcano.
Meanwhile the troop-trains shuttled back and forth in fog,
Lights burned late behind drawn blinds, our ministers met and
    whispered under top hats,
Foundries flared, flames shooting out of dangerous earth.
Presently, amid weakness, sloth, and guile,
The spring came; summer, then; and like ice lasting
Far into summer, the unnatural unseasonable unsafe peace
Crackled at midnight, and still held and held
Beyond suspicion's trial.

How like altering pictures,
How like the changing of images on a screen
Are thought, happening, thing.
Helpless as spectators at a cinema
We watched history unwind from rapid spools,
And in the cafés at dusk, the newsboys crying
Brought the brute fear, sharp as a heart attack.
How we, strangers in the street, stared in each other's faces
With the strained look of lovers parting,
How, lovers, we but glanced and went on, like strangers.
Between our sleep and us the falling dream
Symbolizing utter fear of the future.

Across these ice-fields glittering and unreal,
But truer than the summer shading the streets or rippling before
    the scythe,
Swept actual autumn. And then all at once
All burst asunder.

Asunder.

## II

People under the shadow of a war
Decline from their humanity: the sick beast shows itself,
The pinched mask, the dulled eyes, the shuddering breath,
The animal terribly tamed, now, mute and sweating.
Observe the sluggish crowds, milling feebly
About the bulletins.
                        This boy, drunken, whimpering:
"Here am I; a prostitute and a drunkard
    Made me for lewdness' sake, like a vile cartoon.
    My life has gained me these small coins earned in lavatories.
    Now the bombs offer me equality; I fear it."
This one strapped and fastened into uniform,
Staring: "What do I know of Germany or England?
I am one of the tin toys marching across the pavement,
Once painted as a peasant, now as soldier.
I march toward my terror, since the State has wound me."

This one spectral in the swinging street-light
Coughs: "I am to die for this muck underfoot,
This fatherland, this bog that from my birth
Clogged my footsteps, and now sucks my life."

And this: "Of my country I know only myself,
My wife, my children, and a dozen neighbors,

My pastry-shop, the small room I live in.
I have seen an Englishman perhaps once in my life."
Here at the Ministry, the long halls shine,
The gilded clocks strike twelve, the crystals hang,
The silk hats, polished, wait on the polished table.
Now they come down the marble stairs with their dispatch-cases
As if it were all a newsreel:

                    "Home, good people."

Turn, turn, go home.
                Enter the trap, enter it:
Suspicion makes all wrong, all unfamiliar,
Sharpening the angles of the monstrous room.
The keyhole eavesdrops and the window spies.
Listen: the walls of the great human warren
In stealth prepare their avalanche of stone.

Until, until the bomb imagined falling
Exceeds thought to grow real, falls and bursts,
Splitting the world, filling the world with flames.

Only the mad within their whitewashed cells
Made gentle by violence, or violent still
Twisting within the grasp of giant dreams,
These who suffer, falsely translating thought,
Watch their world grow plausible; at last, confirmed.

"Strangely, these days,
I imagine the Ice-Age, life bogged in frozen filth:
I fear it like the North Pole."
                  "Dark traffic of our cities
Swirling, as if in darkness

Motion of our solid cities thawing,
Our whole ice-solid world like ice resolving."
"Perhaps all this will pass." Perhaps it will.
About our streets deceit, like snow, falls deep.

### III

Almighty God, the spool turns,
Image gives way to image: the Hour advances,
Enters, and is known the Executioner;
Has, too, its cloak, its mask; ascends its stage.
How every animal knows the approach of death!
Man also, shown the axe, the block, now knows it.
As field and woodland were but flowery ways
The beast must travel to the bloody room,
This way our summers and our winters led us,
This way the child's game in the garden, and the bed of love,
The stair ascending and the stair descending,
This way all roads ran, and all signposts pointed.

Asunder.

## Winter Nightfall

January hangs glowing glass
Icicles at eaves and sills.
Day lifts past broken blinds and chimneys,
But high west-spaces glitter yet
And cast such influence beyond night
That folk blaze in the brilliant cold,
And beggars shuffle astral snows;
The cur at street's end, shivering, chill,
Burns in as pure furious light
As stars or absolute Beings wear,
But sniffs a dazzling refuse still.

Now all's of such proud metal wrought,
That lost amid excess of light
The body shivers, not for cold,
But for the vision, winter-bright,
Of radiance bone nor flesh had dulled,
And but a season's penance bought:
Prison and slum and market-square,
As if their substance were but shade,
Glimmer and grow unreal and fade:
The winter lights mount, tier on tier,
As ringed saints on the transpiring stair.

Now the high heavens are like a bell
Repeating peal on peal of light,
But, O, in counterfeit largesse:
These fires though fallen from heaven's height
Will keep no mortal fabric warm,
Nor are of godly gaze begot,
For that divinity is blind
That cannot look on worser things,

But makes all exquisite to its eyes:
Godhead must enter and inform
The sorry shape with Paradise.

And once, they say, it happened so,
But now that wizard's-tale is told.
It, too, ends in mortality,
And what the mortal is, we know.
Though all the heavens compound their fires,
The shades of night close round again,
Like these returning prison-walls.
And though the Child but lately born
Yet fills with radiance all the west,
He perishes at the fall of dusk;
And at the street's end, the dusk falls.

# The Statue

Emblem of fury, caught in immortal storm,
On that quaint-coated back, flung arm, rough arrogant head,
All weathers of all seasons have been shed;
No season, no mortal weather can much harm
A man of metal, whose imperious form
Dazzles, lighting up a century that buried him in its darkness and
thought him dead.

Absolute devotion to a cause
May turn a man wholly to metal, make his whole action and thought
Into a tall tower of passionate pride; transfix him, rapt as he was
For strangers and questioning children to point out;
No matter, for his faith led him; but those who look back and doubt
Leave for their monument a pillar of salt that the first rain topples
and thaws.

What if too stern an ecstasy froze the will
And wrought this rigor in the soul at last?
—The mouth a harsh horn, the staring eyeballs still
Struck with their horrid vision, as though peril were never past?
The metal of his courage, though melted down and recast,
Would thunder as cannon, clang as alarum bell.

He stands too fierce for soft skies: rude, violent, half mad;
Only the hurricane and the earthquake show
The cataclysm for which the hero was bred,
The force that shapes defiance, when, although
All heaven's worst wild-fire streams against his brow,
It wreathes but more terrible a garland of fury for the furious head.

## Horror Story

I think this century a haunted castle
Where history stalks, though dead; the crimes alone
Survive, of all that past; murderer and victim
Puppet-like act their play; are else unknown.

I am the Prince whose reign these dreams usurp,
And heir to all the horrors of this house.
What shall I do? Repair? Or pull down all,
To make some innocent mound where goats may browse?

Alas, I do nothing; sweat, while night turns day
As black guilt turns remorse; as fear, despair;
And shake to hear, O monstrous, O worst of all,
The shapeless Future shambling up the stair.

# The Midnight Meditation

## I

Midnight: I pluck the curtains back, look out
Into a city clouding, silently sinking,
Falling away, fading, engulfed in gloom.

Already ruinous!—the last catastrophe
And final nightfall visibly at hand;
And the wind, now, the wind around a ruin,
Or the wild sea-race through the long sea-halls.

O semblance desolation, seeming is truth:
The city of yesterday that here goes down
Is gone forever, like sunk Lyonesse;

Gone forever as Babylon or Troy
Or towns faint-glimmering that profoundly lie
Drowned in the depths of endless centuries.

## II

Immensity, like the darkness cast from the cloud above
And the darkness earth-born, I am lost in you
Deep as profound towns buried in Time.

I have no mind to mourn with a mournful season,
Mock-mourning of the autumn leaves, of the keening wind,
All savage rites kept by the ancient earth.

I mourn, not grieving, no, at grievous death,
But at the resurgence after death,
And the death again, and senseless resurgence still.

Cycle on cycle, wheeling Infinity,
Boundless Abyss where all things rise and fall,
You are my sickness: the terror of which I dream, and to which
    I awake.

Nightmare phoenix ceaselessly renewed,
Riddling sphinx indifferent to all response,
Paradoxical chimera guarding chaos,

How have you not betrayed us in our journeys,
As the simple immensity of sombre wastes
Turns the lost traveller in a circling track.

Infinity, patient and silent as a beast following,
How subtly have you stalked us in all travels:
Indeed, wherever we went, we were yours at last:

—You, with bones of empires in your craw,
Swallower of whole civilizations, and dainty yet,
Scrupulous still, to capture a lone traveller.

### III

Let children ride the year's sweet carrousel,
Glitter of revolving winter and spring;
We know that faëry wheel and where it takes us.

The illuminated heavens, promising enchantment
Like powerful symbols in a magician's book,
Reveal at last a single simple meaning.

In infinite time the cities burst like rockets, empires gleam and are
   gone,
The bright seas run like quicksilver,
The mountains rear and recede with the waves' motion.

Cloudy Time obscures, yet dulls not so
But fragments of our history survive
To mark how all our action was but motion,
Wind's course, flame's thrust, turnings of the whirlpool.

Patriot, scholar, poet, soldier, saint,
Nothing will eventuate from your anguish:
All faiths and arts are figures on a wheel.

Nothing will come of all these revolutions:
Agonies of the liberator
Prepare new tyranny for new overthrow.

The straight line returns upon itself.
Is infinite, too: all contraries are one.

## IV

I thought once I should have at a man's age
Some wisdom hard and pure as diamond
To make the center of a new steadfast world,

Or some bauble, at least, for a toy—accurate enough
To catch the universe in its gay reflex,
Like Paris reflected in a jewel,

And perhaps after all I have it: at last recognizing
The treadmill as a treadmill: asking of my empty journeys
Nothing, in the end, but to spare my private nobility;

Dwelling at last in a house on the cloudy brink
Where the windows offer no prospect,
And the balconies give on nothing;

Knowing that though we speak with our old sophistry
Of the dawn of hope, the dawn comes endlessly,
Day after trailing day, but our hope never;

As now the new day comes, with its new horrors
Still inert, its tyrannies still voiceless,
And the future rises, like these light-dripping towers,

Like a city rising from the infinite sea.

# On an Adagio by Beethoven

Weep, intransigent mourner, weep,
Weep, and spurn all comforting;
Bitter is the fate of man,
Nor is it altered by your woe;
But sorrow being ennobled so,
And salt tears to such sweetness wrought,
The angels doomed to Paradise
Envy us our suffering.

# The Mirror Men

A muffled clang announced catastrophe
Like a play's beginning; there was the Castle; he entered,
Breathlessly barred the door.—Now safe at last?
Shut from his enemies?—Alas, no; trapped; at bay.

—Phantoms in the candleshine? the usual
Living portraits of the haunted castle?
—Mirrors; mirrors everywhere; in each,
Like puppet in his cabinet, his reflection.
Selves, selves beyond number, mocked with dumbshow antic
His agony and fright; all, all with faces
Lugubrious and absurd as tragic masks.

—What? He could not distinguish Self and World?
Not Same and Other?—No; could not distinguish.

—Nevertheless was noble? The Knight was knightly,
His Lordship lordly?
                        —Not so; the great castle
Grew false and tawdry as an opera set
And shrank to the old house where he was born;
The ancestral armor became football uniforms,
The arms but a boy's trophies, sticks and nests.
Outside, the tragic world, moon, branch, and snow,
Changed also; the moon cold and ridiculously large,
Like a boy's dream of a giant snowball; beyond, the mountains,
Enormous ads for ice-cream. "Childhood again," he thought,
"And madness, like winter, simplifies the world
To Black and White; but nothing reduces all;
A basic Opposition still remains."

—What then? He fought? Drew the bright sword and fought,
Vanquished the phantoms, or was bravely slain,
Slain by his reflection in a glass?

—Ah, no; the sword was gone; he climbed the stair.

—The mirror men still followed?—Followed still,
Past the chessboard with the unfinished game
Netted in spiderweb; past the table with cards
That should have spelt out fortune, and were used for solitaire,
Up stair, to tower—no, to attic—room.

—What did the Knight, then?—Stared at his childhood bed,
That ship whose only port was a bad dream;
And saw, at last, his shadow on the wall.

—Then, then was free? Grew brave?—Ah no, ah no;
All fears reduce, he thought, to a child's shadow,
All friends, enemies, strangers, to one's self;
And suddenly saw the carvings: door, bed, table, chair
Emblemed with snakes devouring themselves;
And stared, and shook with horror; at last crept
Silently into the bed and hid his eyes;

—And then?—Then, holding its hands before its face,
The clock, shuddering, struck, sounding the hour,
Over and over again the self-same hour
Too late for action and too black for hope.

## Childe Roland, Etc.

Certainly there was something to their stories:
Something had been at the fields, the pond *was* shaped
Like an enormous footprint; there were the usual signs,
Small herds, snapped trees.
I sat astride my horse in the autumn twilight,
Conscious of looking well; they crowded about me,
Jabbering, gesticulating, spilling out of straw-thatched huts.
Later, outside the tavern, I was shown
A number of women—all, it was said, deflowered.

Well, I set out at once: the approach was sinister,
Full of the usual obstacles; suddenly,
There was the castle. I was just about to knock
—Thunderously, of course—when the door opened.
I think I have never met a more charming person.
True, he was ugly, and—*large;* but he had a manner.
You know how personality makes up for so much!
He gave me cocktails, followed by an excellent supper;
I felt ridiculously clumsy in my clanking armor.
Later, with coffee and brandy, I had the facts.
Land and cattle were his; the people were squatters.
He did not resent the trespassing and depredation,
But thought it a pity they felt so possessive.
He read me his poems, humbly took my suggestions,
Played some things of Chopin's rather well.
I left quite late, somewhat reluctantly,

And went back with the thought of punishing the villagers,
But they had already begun their singing and dancing;
My ears rang with it several miles beyond.
Later, "he had eaten six men"; that very day

I had a little note from him—half invitation,
Half begging the name of a competent attorney.

My armor stands in the hall; I often think of my ancestors.
Was it different for them?
Nowadays, I observe, poetry is chiefly lyrical.

## *Poem*

O lands shift, grass grows, moon rots, wind
Blows: the statue, broken, furnishes the sling;
Till the beast stares at high memorials fallen.

Then towns are grains, and the sun will light the theater of the
    rocks,
The robed waves, like a tragic chorus, move
Still in the slow dance over sea-caves, sea-graves, sea-mountains,
    sunken empires;

Thunder and wind shall keep their ceremonies,
The rain its ritual; the seasons in solemn passage
Perform their antique mysteries, unprofaned:

Signifying that the Earth remains the Earth,
Patiently having suffered our harsh history,
The weight of our ponderous cities, the wounds of our wars.

## Ballad of the Scarecrow Christ

"My son, come pierce my soul with a sword,
  Scrape death from these bones,
  Build them into a gay cathedral,
  It will sing in all its stones.

"All the carved angels and holy images
  Will sing, to cymbal and psaltery,
  Till the long winter of Eden ends,
  And Christ lies easy on his Cross,
  And the Cross turns into a Tree."

O Christ hangs high upon the Cross,
The cathedral glitters as if afire,
But demons glare from coign and finial,
Couple with the gargoyles, howl in the choir.

Farewell, cries the son, to the crow-roost scarecrow,
Farewell to a country curst with foul crows,
Take ship and sail from this haunted land,
No Garden is hidden beneath these snows.

O see the angry wanderer:
It is his breath in the sail
Drives him alone through a world of waters
In a ship of his own will.

Look, look! amid what pomp of waters
He lordly rides like the light of day;
All the sea-robed waves throng round,
Sea-foam garlands all his way,

O see the sleek sea-people raining with jewels,
The salt-blue flashing with fin, with wing!
Continents rear from the sea at his coming,
Foaming into instant spring,

Amorous, the hills bend toward him,
Hanging gardens kiss his hand,
Ocean murmurs in lamentation
As his foot summers all the land.

O all the air is sharp with spires
O all the air bubbles with domes
O all the air is afloat with palaces
Towering terraces
Fountains and peacocks on all the terraces
And brilliant millions on all the terraces
And the dead burst singing from their tombs
Singing singing the living and the dead
Spires domes palaces terraces
And stairs stairs the tallest tower
Candles flowers a feast is laid.
Now. Now. A feast laid.

O what is this festival, what the feast,
What is this host, what this homage?
Millions millions smiling millions:
And every one of them his image.

All faces are his mirrored face,
Whether the living or the dead;
And for that long banquet laid
Cups blaze with his blood, his body is the bread.

Candles quiver and smoke,
O the sky runs wild, the air turns brown,
Every building rocks and walks
And cracks to cascades roaring down,

Air mutters and glares and then goes black;
Pursued by a million cannibal images
Down, down the great stair of the terraces
He is running running like a man afire
With a lightning-bolt at his back.

Noah alone on the bulging flood
He sails to drown a million selves
But the Ark heaves him into a hissing and hackled
Green-black ocean that boils and halves

And spews him Jonah to a far dim shore
And the land turns horseback to hurl him off;
Forests wither, stones singe and shriek;
Fire, water, flee him like the wind;
Towers and houses shrink aside;
Look, look; Judas, without kin or kind.

Every puddle pukes to see him,
Every rivulet coils and strikes;
Crawling over quaking mountains and valleys
(Husks, husks) like an old volcano
He rages to retch soul-fires: fails.
He oozes in sewers, dogs drop him in alleys.

Now all the aureoled saints and martyrs
Had breathed but one breath of eternal bliss
And the damned who dance the dance of the burning
Had screamed for twelve eternities

And so much earthly time had passed
As turns green forests into coal
And that coal into diamond
And that diamond into dust:

Now in a stark field without stalk
In a country of cold slag
Too poor for hour or season
Too starved for crow or hawk

O what is that on its knees
And what is that in darkling air?
A hanged man there?
No, no:

Anybody could,
Anyone can
With a rag or two and a cross of wood
Make an image of man:
It is a scarecrow.

"If for insulted suffering
Other suffering may atone,
Lie easy on your cross of wood,
I perish on my cross of bone.

And what if all suffering be in vain?
I honor still that agony:
Christ or Judas, each in pain,
Perished upon a bitter tree."

O see, see: he stands
In a vast hollow like the inside of a mountain
Arch on arch
A Church
(Is it a bell that rings? Who brings
All these flames? Who sings?
Can it be that stone sings?)

—All the carved angels and holy images
Sing, to cymbal and psaltery,
And the long winter of Eden ends,
And Christ lies easy on his Cross,
And the Cross turns into a Tree.

## Plot Improbable, Character Unsympathetic

I was born in a bad slum
Where no one had to die
To show his skeleton.
The wind came through the walls,
A three-legged rat and I
Fought all day for swill.
My father was crazed, my mother cruel,
My brothers chopped the stairs for fuel,
I tumbled my sisters in a broken bed
And jiggled them till all were dead.
Then I ran away and lived with my lice
On my wits, a knife, and a pair of dice,
Slept like a rat in the river reeds,
Got converted fifty times
To fifty different creeds
For bowls of mission broth,
Till I killed the grocer and his wife
With a stove-poker and a carving-knife.
The mayor said, Hang him high,
The merchants said, He won't buy or sell,
The bishop said, He won't pay to pray.
They flung me into a jail,
But I, I broke out,
Beat my bars to a bell
Ran all around the town
Dingling my sweet bell,
And the mayor wanted it for his hall,
The merchants wanted to buy it,
The bishop wanted it for his church,
But I broke my bell in two,
Of one half a huge bullet made,
Of the other an enormous gun,

Took all the people of all the world
And rolled them into one,
And when the World went by
With a monocle in his eye,
With a silk hat on his head,
Took aim and shot him dead.

# The Night There Was Dancing in the Streets

More paper blackened with more signatures;
Top-hats and handshakes, smiles of dry-toothed diplomats,
Crowds, drums, flags, cannon, fireworks, torchlight processions.
Truce, peace, alliance,
What matter, what matter?
                              Close the windows, now,
Light the lamp, and read Thucydides

Who knew that passion and character of a nation
Stemmed from far causes; poverty of the soil
Brought safety; safety, growth—eventual greatness;
Habit of growth, ambition; the quick Athenian
Was his own land's best harvest, and so flourished.
Conversely, now, richness of earth brought war,
Stunting increase, and the sullen Spartan
Sank man in soldier; the armor moulded the man.
Thus power and fear of power grew side by side,
Contrary blossoms out of contrary earths;
There lay the principles of war; meanwhile, let run,
Let rhetors roar and heralds strut, let town
Quibble with town; the tough root turns all axes,
The fruits of Necessity ripen in all weathers.

# Elegy  *(In mem. Dr. P. F. S.)*

Here, amid landscape
Austere as the cold profile of the dead,
No mark. O, but remembrance is a mark.

Surgeon, painter, traveller, hunter, friend,
Bone-chalk: saw once too often
The wintry sun come to the wintry earth
Like the impotent bridegroom to the frigid bride.

Vanished; the flesh
Snatched like a cloth; the spirit palmed, pocketed,
Magician's trick-Jack, quicksilver Merlin
Fled through a cup's crack, hidden in a hair's hollow;
Was the live man, then, only
Illusion of the wizard's cabinet?

Is the skull, then, the real? The vivid face, its mask?
Death the one mummer, masking in all forms?
Fair world, I trod your lands, I sailed your seas,
Prince of your phantom palaces, never guessing
What dungeons beneath cloudy towers, beneath
Fountains and gardens, peacock terraces,
And avenues of the lily-drifting swan,
Dark of the beast's den, bone-littered.
Fool of vanity! Caught, like a lark, with mirrors;
Tricked, by the hypocrite rose.
Here at the grave's edge I stand, on the hair-trigger trap-door;
The Sphinx of death, maw crammed, and ravenous still,
Reads me her riddle: now answer true, or die.

Plato's ghost cries from the mental North,
"My Pole is safe beyond your flashing seasons;
The Equation lasts; what matter what is equal?"

—I sailed that Arctic void, up world-side; there, world's crystal
      boneyard, saw with mind's-eye
Color's invisible Essence, absolute Aurora
Springing from splintered spar, staining all stuffs,
Dark shattering into light, light into color; O extreme North no
      north,
The mind like compass crazed with North, North only,
And there not growth nor habitation; Death.
That One is none. One Point, no line. Illusion of depth in mirrors.

And now the toy-world tin-man, wound up, whines
"These cogs are cogs; wheel and wheel's motion only."
—Why, squirrel's wheel, even rat's treadmill—! Death again.

Better crude doves, chipped angels bearing hopes.
Shall these stones fly?—"So he passed over,
And all the trumpets sounded on the other side."
Alas! His children's children following
Found, not the River, but the Abyss; and asking

"O Grave—? O Death—?" were answered: "Here."

O Christ, Christ named often. Now, first time, called.

Now in old masters, angels on a cloud
Have, with their beards and nightshirts,
The look of shipwrecked mariners on a raft:

*The Ark's wrecked!* Thorns crackle, but I drown.
Laugh at old Bible cuts, look out to see,
Actual, above the actual town,
Sailing in slow flight from street to street,
Stilly moving as a cloud that in calm weather traverses the whole
      heaven without disarrangement,

Stretched wings, every feather distinct, long sable garments trailing,
     slim feet trailing, the long hands lightly grasping
The urn pouring slowly down voluminous fumes
Falling silently upon the tall coffer-like houses and the lifted faces,
The Angel of Pestilence.
          All death, death.

Submit. Submit. Walls fall. Enter the Conqueror:
Where's Tamburlaine? Why, there's no one; at the gate
A starving dog lurks to gnaw my bones.

An end, at least.
Not weep, no. No more asking and answering,
The question like a blow, the response like blood.
Into your grave I fall, am dead with you.
—The first night's cold. The grave leaks. Now, dog Death.
What, bone-dust so quickly? Disperse it, then.
And then what? Nothingness?
        No: sown seed.

O, die, was it? Suffer death, descend,
Hear, in the grave, that pulse? Fathom that mystery
How furiously life rages till it lives,
Turns the brute rock into, the wild air into,
The very clay of the grave's pit into
Bird, beast, flower, and tree?

O miracle of this puppet on three strings:

Believe, because my fabric. As I see
Because my being is seeing.
        Break, memory, break:
Who recalls the future?
        Peace, poor ghost.

# Jack-in-the-Box

Devil sprang from box,
Frightening the children, who would not be comforted.
In vain they were wooed with all the other toys;
Expecting new terror, they would not look or listen; like an angry
    demon
Their fear ran round the house, from room to room.
At last their mother led them off to bed.

Allison lit his pipe; forgot it, thinking.
Something more had been released
Than long-necked Punch, nodding and leering still.
As in the ancient casuistry of Eden,
Falsehood, accepted, falsified all truth;
All the old pleasant facts now fell away,
Flimsy as Christmas wrappings; there was the house, now.
Pretty with snows, with candy roofs and sills,
Sparkling and false as the hut in the fairy tale;
As if in a haunted forest shone the tree,
With fruits—pear, apple, plum—all poison-bright.
Outside the wind swept away the Christmas illusion, raising a white
    fog
Where toys like Martians stalked, destroying all.

He thought: how simply terror can enter a house.
The angel, treed, was trembling, that had promised peace.

# The Son of the Enemy

"It was the ring."

                              "Your engagement ring?"
  The clock ticked, the long flames
  Fled up the chimney.
                              "One she'd stolen."
"Stolen?"
                    "At least, I thought she had;
  It belonged to Lucy."
                              "Lucy—Blythe?"
"Yes; at the funeral I saw it
  On Lucy's hand; Isbel touched her,
  Sobbed once, I thought; then she had it,
  Tried to hide it; afterwards
  Said it had fastened on her finger.
  I found that—odd. We had words."

"You haven't seen her?"
                              "No one has;
  She acts as if she had the plague."

"This ring—what's it look like?"
                              "A plain band,
  Dark metal, old; some writing on it.
  —They say that Lucy acted this way;
  What was wrong with Lucy, Father?"

"Wrong?"
                    "I mean, more than just her—illness."
  I saw in the fire a greater burning.

"It wasn't—illness."

                    He stiffened; then—

"What of her child?"

                      "It was not a child."

That year a decaying season
Lingered into late December,
Would not be cleansed; old laws were altering.

## II

It might have been a dog at the door,
But wasn't; I got him to the couch,
Got brandy down him, and stood staring
At the torn clay-daubed clothes, the knees
And palms skinned raw, the anguished face
Of a spent runner.

                  A wind raved,
Frantic for something in the house.
I left him so; before the crucifix,
For the first time almost doubted prayer;
Then his eyes were watching me.

"Can you speak?"

                He nodded.

                    "In God's name, tell me—"

"I went; she wouldn't let me in;
Then *it* came at me, and I ran—
I *ran!*"

                My closed eyes saw him run
In moon-dusk through the stricken woods,

A horror at his back.
                              "That 'child'—
Did you see it, Father? Was it dead?"

"Yes. I saw it. It was dead."

"What was it, then?"
                              "I do not know."
He shuddered; stood. "I'm going back."

"I'll go with you."
                              No wind, now;
The stillness something like held breath.

### III

We pleaded at that obdurate door
Like souls at Judgment.
                              "Break it down."
He hurled his fury; I stepped through
The smashed frame, lifting book and cross,
And was thrown instantly to my knees;
And he, too, grappling it, was down,
One arm sheared off already.
                              She, then,
Erect upon the stair, she knew
The one way out of this; her hand
Clutched a thing that roared and roared,
Without one flash, and fell. The ring
Ran at my feet; I snatched it up;
Then there was silence.
                              My faith had failed;
They had their human victory,
But lay like soldiers on the field.

## IV

"I too, I too shall send among you
A Son begotten on your clay;
For what He does, that I can do."
I spelled that out, and dropped the ring
Into the jar; stood looking out
The window while the acid seethed.
Autumn had ended; flakes were falling;
Bells chimed; in the whitening square
A great green cone rose glittering;
Men on ladders strung festoons;
Children stood watching.
                All safe; safe;
But barely spared a stranger Birth.

# The Pole

Sail, pretty sailor, in your charming ship
That always finds the weathers you like best
And continents that shape themselves to please you
And waves that only hold bright mirrors up.
Sail round and round your little pretty world
With all its islands looking as you might,
Were you an island; with birds, beasts, and flowers
So exquisitely shaped, so gaily colored
You yourself might have made them; and so you have.
Sail on, and play your mandolin, and sing;
You are the lone enchanted listener.
Sail on, for soon or late the summons comes:
One night you will wake to an odd twang,
With others echoing, as one by one
The strings (how very odd!) of your mandolin
Part, with a sound you never heard before.
Then the light craft will quiver; like a floating needle
Swing trembling round, to point in the one direction
You somehow never took, though you wanted to;
Oddly as that, the adventure will begin.
At first you may be pleased by the unusual;
Queer, how fast the ship moves, without wind.
There will be so much that is pretty, too:
Clear darkling air, such extraordinary stars,
And hour after hour under the quivering arch
Of rapid lights, the wind-ruffled corona,
The streams, pennons, oriflammes, thunder-bolts of light;
And the colors, the colors; the bright shadows of the ship,
Blue beam of Arctic iceberg, red searchlight ray
Of heart of ice-mountain, clean depth-of-diamond green;
So much, so much that is pretty; though perhaps
One might regret a little the broken glass

Ice-fields, and the wild white frightening mountains,
And that obvious touch, snow bears who sit and fish,
Or swim in the black lustrous water between floes.
So much, so much indeed, that before you know it
The ship jams fast amid ice-blocks, and there,
Amid great broken prisms and piled spar,
Sparkles the Pole, the vast Axle, visible at last.
It is then you will suddenly know it: the true North,
Where all gay hues resolve to the one white,
And all directions terminate; the simple North
Implicit in all the complex wanderings;
The pin-point truth, amid a world of fictions,
That cannot be transmuted or denied;
And knowing it, you will also know the wind,
The ravenous sleet, the brute dark, the raging cold,
The terror of a world that is not you.

# The Four Black Bogmen

O she took the babe still slick from the waterbag,
Bathed it and swathed it and cradled it then
In a willow basket and carried it
Through the pit-black woods to a fog-roofed fen.
There amid plashy ferns she laid it
And watched the slug-black ooze slip in.

An old man rose from the smoking rushes:
"O why do you walk on the tipover tussocks
And heaving hummocks of slippery quags?
Think twice when you do what you came to do
Or the four black bogmen who set such snags
Will track you down and switch shapes with you.

"Every one of the four is a sharp shape-trader
Who can look like a toad or a bubble in the bog,
A snipe on a stick or a snail on a stalk,
A worm in a web or a bead in the fog."
"O how do you know, you old swamp-squatter?"
"I am the first." And he grabbed, and he had her.

O she watched as he swanked in her shape through the swamp,
Then shaky and old, she hobbled away
Till she tripped on the roots of a big-toed stump
And there as she stuck, the slick roots quickened,
Slipped round like blacksnakes, that trap of a tree
Hissed in her ear, "I am the second."

O a bad shape sat in her sticks like a bird,
Yet what could trouble a root-rotten tree?
Through the misty forest stumbled a rickety
Cripple of a leper, bagging wood,
Who clutched at a branch as if to break it; the
Lipless mouth said, "I am the third."

O now on a leper's pegs she pottered
To stop her trick in the nick, if she could;
In the snake-black mire, in the coiling mud,
There was the child, choking in muck.
O how she snatched, how she cuddled! It shuddered,
Clung with its bog-black claws, and spoke.

## Able, Baker, Charlie, Et Al.

The grass hissed, then
Power and phone lines broke,
Cocoanuts flew like cannonballs,
Palm trees bent double, and most snapped,
Tin roofs took off and scaled about,
Slashed legs or arms or heads from all they met.
The shacks went somersaulting this way and that, like tumbleweeds,
The coffee industry blew out like a match.
One house, to show what it could do,
Got up from its foundations and waddled off,
As if sick of everything, turned back to lumber;
A second committed suicide; jumped from the cliff.
A whole wood thought it was time that the world saw its roots,
And showed them, leaping up into the air
And staying there, locked into a fantastic arch
You can still walk under. One family
Cowering in the cellar, heard a fearful crash
And learned, next day, they had an extra roof
(The one who had lost it knew about it sooner).
Another found that fish can fly in flocks,
Given reason enough. Robertson and his friends,
Groping in the dark of boarded windows,
Groped from room to room as something removed
Room after room; ended up packed tight, bolt-upright in the tiny
    kitchen,
Twenty-three persons, four kids standing in the kitchen sink
Of a house that had shrunk to a kitchen.
The boats in the harbor really caught it; all but the big freighter
Listened to their anchors,
Got convinced it was no wetter at the bottom
And a heck of a lot safer; so they went to it.

Robertson, squinting out a crack in the shutter
Through absolutely horizontal rain
At a vegetable world writhing with pain, and shrieking with it, too,
Saw a funny thing: one old moth-eaten cow, left out in a field,
Knew she was trapped, turned her rump to the source of the trouble,
Braced legs, and stood that way through the whole business,
Though her bags slapped the tar out of her sides, and vice versa.
Next morning, at least she was there, and damn little else was,
The green had even been knocked out of the grass, as if autumn had
    come
(A thing it never does). Robertson thought,
There's more hell than anything, what you pick up in one jam
Might work in the next; he got three things out of this one:
First, that when everything behaves unnaturally,
The cause is still natural; secondly,
The fools who go out in the lull get hit by the second installment;
The third he got from the cow; it has nothing to do with patient
    endurance of difficulties,
But is somewhat indecent; at least, he puts it indecently;
And it mayn't save you, but it will relieve your feelings.

# *Crucifix*

Here is this silver crucifix, to recall
Immortal agony: the mortality of the immortal;
Christ crucified again, but painlessly, in effigy;
All wrought to grace; anguish translated to beauty, suffering feigned
    in calm silver.
Look at this, then think of the actual scene:
Friday, Friday the thirteenth, as some think,
Hot and bright at first, but gradually darkening and chilling;
The rock and sway of a great packed crowd,
A crowd like any other that comes to witness executions,
With market-baskets and bundles and purses and other tokens of lives
    that would be resumed
After this interruption; a crowd with children and dogs
Crawling in and out through the forest of legs.
Think of the straining, the craning to see as hammers and nails
Behaved after the fashion of hammers and nails,
Though the nails went through veins and flesh and wedged bones
    apart.
And then the cross raised, the third of that day, displaying to all eyes
(Eyes glittering or sombre, lust-lit or horror-struck, but mostly
    curious)
The head, turning slowly from side to side,
As always with the pinned or the impaled,
The eyes already rapt with suffering,
The hands nailed like frogs to the rough cross-timber,
The feet spiked to the foot-block; amid cries and murmurs
The cross raised; and after a little while,
The eyes of the spectators straying, their lips beginning to discuss
    other executions, and other things than executions,
The crowd slowly dispersing, the best parts being over,
Leaving only a few whispering at the foot of the cross in the gathering
    dark, and the Roman soldiers,

To whom this was another execution,
Glad to relax after the anxieties of maintaining discipline.

Think of the terrible solitude of the Cross:
Of that body shuddering (for it was a body)
And the knees buckling, as they would, till straightened convulsively
In the drag of the body's weight on the hands and the aching armpits,
And again and again buckling and straightening, again and again
   throughout the long day, as weakness overcame pain, and pain,
   weakness,
And the painful thirst of the wounded, worse than the wounds,
And the flies, to whom Christ's blood was as any other,
And worse than all, the fear, the increasing fear
That all had been illusion, save this pain, this death
(For we think that none, not even God, may put on the man-shape
   and not feel this fear)
And this in the terrible solitude of the Cross.

Think of this, gaze your fill on it, then remember
It is the Christ that sanctifies the Cross,
Not the Cross, Christ; and remember, it is not
Preëminence in pain that makes the Christ
(For the thieves as well were crucified)
No, but the Godhead; the untouchable unguessable unsuffering
Immortality beyond mortality,
Which feigns our mortality as this silver feigns it,
And of which we are ignorant as that multitude;
For the pain comes from the humanity; the pain we know;
The agony we comprehend; of the rest, know nothing.

## First Death, Second Death, and Christ Crucified

"Because his face glassed yours, yet could not keep such feature,
  But must mark a snake's mask there,
  Blasting that garden, bush and tree,
  Now let me scourge him front and back,
  Flay vein and flesh until he glasses me,
  And learns with what despair
  The silent bone can rage
  Till it is dust of dust
  To glass the serpent's track."

"Since his face must glass yours, yet cannot keep such feature,
  And since your dark is darkness of my fire,
  His body being the darkness of his soul,
  Flay it front and back,
  But give that other into my control,
  To blaze within my garden all afire
  And learn what lightnings blast
  The flames, there, where all craters
  Glass me, and burn black."

"Because my face glassed his, yet must not keep such feature,
  Even that suffering dust is dear,
  And since its suffering glasses mine,
  I sweeten lash and fire,
  And from that garden's blasted tree, declare
  Gardens shall spring up where that suffering passed,
  Eden shall be wherever gardens are,
  And you and you and he
  Shall glass my face at last."

# The Fountain

The marble watergod amid waterlights
Utters cold mysteries from unmoving lips,
Water-language, bubbling syllables, a water-voice murmuring

As if to say: I, this mercurial element,
Was wave and cloud; the rainbow, and the rain;
Fire at the icicle's heart, heart's-blood of the rose;
And am and shall be all again.

I am a heaven for cloud-slow swans to sail,
An abyss, a raging gulf, a monster-pit;
A mirror wherein each thing sees its image;

I become whatever drinks of me, bird, beast, flower;
Nevertheless I am none of these, am myself alone, without shape or
    color,
But tomb and cradle, One and Many, variable and eternal;
You will never comprehend me: Come, drink.

# PART IV

# The Exegesis

Nothing is lost; be still; the universe is honest.
Time, like the sea, gives all back in the end,
But only in its own way, on its own conditions:
Empires as grains of sand, forests as coal,
Mountains as pebbles. Be still, be still, I say;
You never were the water, only a wave;
Not substance, but a form substance assumed.
Have you forgotten?—Saturn (that is, Time)
Devoured all his children except four,
Pluto, Juno, Neptune, Jove, these being
—Why, antiquity knew it—earth, air, water, fire.

## Wild Horse

I have struggled all day with a thought like a wild noble horse
To make it tread to the measure of a verse;

Now I give over—Tamed, what should it be, after all
But a beast of burden, or a sight for the carnival?

Let it go, let it run free, to be seen only by those who can follow in
    its perilous track,
Or if it must be ridden at last, let it bear a hero on its back.

## For a Friend Defeated

Be still; let them mock.
Lie there in the dust,
Study what the earth
Beneath the Himalayas
Can bear because it must.
Learn silence now and learn
Silence from the fern
That, bitterly oppressed,
Still stamps its delicate frond
In the oppressing rock.

# The Altar

I found the ruined altar in the glen,
Nearly returned, now, to brute natural rock.
A bush blazed on it, like an altar-fire.

A shrine cast down as by an enemy;
Its coronals and garlands broken away,
Its columns fallen, shattered; all as if
The only carvers had been wind and rain.

A bitter token: that faith, that labor spurned.
I stood remembering how the robed priestly waves
Chant in strange processionals, and the wild earth
Year after year renews mysterious rites
To powers that make no covenant with man,

Gods barbarous and implacable, that destroy
Even what we would consecrate to them,
And only in shrines made pure of us at last
Place for themselves a proud offering of their own.

## The Cry

Martin, the telegram trembling in his hand,
Walked out upon the porch; went down the stairs.
He heard her call out, "Anything from Johnnie?"
But for the moment could not speak; suddenly
He had to sit, or fall; so he sat down,
On the last step.
               Strange—at such a time—to notice
A butterfly. Just out of its cocoon;
It lay upon a sun-warmed stone, moved feebly
Wings that in minutes, doubtless, would unfold
To full perfection; a thing so delicate
It was difficult to think that the same power
That made the enormous suns had made this too,
Done more than that—equipped, adorned it, even,
As if all God's care and labor since Creation
Had been to build and cherish this one thing.

Suddenly a jay swept down, and had it.

Martin leaped up, brain ringing with the cry
The butterfly might have cried out; the huge scream
Echoed and re-echoed without end
Since first the stronger pinned the weaker down,
Ages back, in the awakening slime:
The cry of horror and agony, the fierce indictment
Of the Creator by the created thing
Tricked into a universe of fright.
He felt within his breast that bitter cry
Bubble up like blood. He uttered it.

## A Farewell

Farewell, who would not wait for a farewell;
Sail the ship that each must sail alone;
Though no man knows if such strange sea-farers
Fare ill or well,
Fare well:

Learn, if you must, what they must learn who sail
The craft that must sink; sail, till the tall cloud
Is closer to the keel than that far floor,
And to those deepest deeps descend, go down;
Though you fare ill, you yet fare well, to be
King of an empty empire's kingdom come,
Amid the ruins and treasures of that sea;

Learn, if you fare well,
There in the last apocalypse of the waves
What twilights deepen on the drowned man drifting
Atlantiswards, what hues light herons' wings
Aloft in sunset skies when earth is dark,
What unheard chords complete all music's close,
When, fierce as rubies in the vein-dark mine,
The lit blood blazes as the brain goes black;

Last jewel of all the world of light, until
The kingdom come of greater light, and death of night, and death
Of Death, that shall also die,
If all fare well.

# A Nocturnal for His Children

Night after night, alone,
My daughters and my son,
I ponder the starry sky,
The Book of Heaven, with all
Its burning charactery,
Its scripture of suns and moons,

I watch the seas unroll
Again and again their scroll,
I brood upon the runes
In the mountain-folds
And the words graven in the hills

Till dazzled and full of shame
Dull scholar that I am
I turn away at last
Knowing I cannot read
One word, one character
Of what is written there.

No man, my children, none,
Can read one word of it
Or with certainty attest
Even to meaning there.
Through passionate voices cry
That all spells out one Name,
They are only men who cry,
They are only such as I.
The Riddle is still unguessed.

Though saint and martyr rejoice
In agony and death
So their last bitter breath

May testify, they only
Testify to their faith:
Jesus called out on the cross,
There was no answering voice.

The universe is vast:
Winging to span such space,
A star must fail, as a bird
Fails, and falls into the sea
(And still there is sea, and sea.)
Yet this, for all we know
May be one atom within
A universe vaster still
And in one mote of dust
Worlds within worlds may spin.

Between abyss and abyss,
Two infinities,
All men must walk; but blest
And twice blest are they
Who see the great vortices
Of turning worlds and the least
Atoms of the least atom obey
The perpetual command
Of the silent voice; who find
On all things the visible mark
Of the invisible hand:
They know both good and ill
Execute one will;
Gazing at night, they see
Star after star, where we
See void, and infinite dark:

The Tables of the Law
Are delivered them; they know
Winter as a sign
Of Eden returning like spring.
Frost shall keep them warm,
And the hurricane not harm;
No storm but shall bring its Bow
Of Covenant that no Flood
Shall come but they have an Ark.
Though they walk in deserts and furnaces
Flames and lions to them
Shall glitter harmless as flowers.
And if they weep or bleed
Every drop of their blood
Every tear they shed
Burns as one jewel more
Of treasures laid up in heaven.
All things shall be to them
As a cloud or a pillar of fire
To lead them till at last
Death opens to them like the Red
Sea, and thus they pass
From bondage to safety and peace.

Others, not led but driven,
Driven, my children, see
The universe like a fire
Raging out of control
And all things are its fuel;
A fire that warms nothing,
Lights nothing, is purposeless,
But its flames must storm and storm

Till all is consumed, and it dies.
Even were it the altar-fire
Of the True God, they cry,
What should such sacrifice
Avail the faggots that burn?
And as they speak they see
All altars ruined at last
All temples overthrown
By powers that spare not,—spurn,
Indeed—even their own.

And there are those who find
Design, but behold the lamb
Fashioned cunningly
And the lion as cunningly
Devised to strike it down;
All creatures furnished, equipped
But as the Emperor
Arms the gladiator.
Monster and monster contend;
Blood-made, and mad for blood,
The nightmare foetus forms
Within the womb of fright
Till all kill all in the end.

My children, I cannot tell
Which of these is right.
I never heard God's voice,
To me no angels descend.
All I know is my soul
Which is, like this night sky,
Far more dark than bright,

Yet in that dark waste
While I watch out its night
All strives from dark to light:

Not knowing false from true,
I yet know good from bad;
I cannot think my God
Worse than myself: I
Demand a nobler faith:

I say that pain and death
Are of small account
Beside life and joy;
But each singular soul,
All that is born, is torn,
As were these galaxies,
From one Substance; rent,
It cannot be content
Till it rejoin the whole;
Nor is there principle of
Such union, except love;

Not in God's image was man
First created, but in
Likeness of a beast;
Until that beast became man,
All travailled in death and pain
And shall travail still
Till man be the image of God
And nothing shall transform
Man to that image, but love;
And this I believe is God's will.

And all shall work that Will:
Planet and planet shall spin,
Atom and atom, until
The scriptures of heaven and earth,
Mountain and ocean, spell
The one unnameable Name
Of One we know nothing of,
Save what we learn from love,
Love that has one name only
Since love makes all things one

As it makes us one,
My daughters and my son.

## Entertainment for a Traveller

Suddenly, any day now, it must come
Silently into your bedroom, and there stand
Monstrous, ponderous, black with bolted mail,
Reeking hot metal and oil; the huge headlight
A trumpet-blast of brilliance, breaching the dark.
Make your farewells, remembering how all
Departures are so very much like death.
Farewell to all friends: bed, glass, basin, chair,
The crack in the ceiling that could leak bad dreams,
And that odd country of which you never were
Quite certain: was it some bedclothes-landscape
Or were those indeed dingy snow-slopes, where
Rough pines, erect as bears, put out their paws?
No matter; mount; as you move down the aisle
Observe all the pale still passengers
Wearing masks of meditation or of sleep.
Now one moment while the engine strains
Like pounding heart and bursting lungs, and then
A wrench of starting, as if strong chains had snapped.
Enter your compartment; remark the odors
—Wax, oak, rosewood, certain depressing perfumes.
On every curve, look back—if possible—
At the long slow cortège of following cars
Before the dark file straightens, buckles down
To climb the endless ladder of the rails.
Ignore the lit billboards, the redlights throbbing anxiously;
Their allurements or alarms are not for you;
Only observe how soon the world outside
Resumes its business, after the brief interruption
Occasioned by your passing. Should this not amuse you,
All journeys afford excellent opportunities
For contemplation; contemplate, if you will,

How swiftly vanishes a world thought steadfast,
Towns, fields, villages, swept off into darkness,
All designs woven by your earlier journeys
Rapidly unravelling. As down rushing rails
The train streaks like a rocket-sled, roars through hollow mountains,
Sweeps over vast trestles spanning oceans,
—Grows taut with speed, grows weightless at last with speed,
Grows still at last with speed—you will find yourself meditating
Your previous deportment; assessing your will, your courage;
Measuring, to a hair, the merit of your love.
Doubtless you will find all to your satisfaction.
If, not, you must meditate further (knowingly or not,
You have put on your own mask of meditation).
Ponder a darkness where one by one the lights
Expire, like the last thoughts in a dying brain,
And reflect that, whatever the case, you need not hurry;
You have time to invent the most plausible excuses.

# *In Defense of Superficiality*

Respect all surfaces. The skater is
Safe until his superficiality
Fails. A bridge, the frailest,
Is better than the abyss. The green earth's pleasant,
*Very* pleasant, isn't it? Don't dig.
Friendship and love are surfaces. Respect them.

All surfaces are smooth seas, and the ship
Moves to music, the sea is shimmering strings,
The sun strums golden wires, and the wind sings,
All mariners must be dancers to such minstrelsy,
Until the prow too curious probes too deep
And music ends and light ends but the sea
Goes on and on and in the whirlpool's round
The dancers go on dancing without sound.

Accept this final bubble,
From one drowned.

# The Cocks of Babylon

"Every particle of the universe
  Was forged to outlast eternities;
  Not one can be destroyed, not one;
  Is the spirit less than these?"
  Cried the cocks of Babylon.

"Such subtle threads bind Age and Age
  As bear the soul through nerve and bone;
  What shall Death borrow, thieve, or beg?"
  Cried the cocks of Babylon,
  Crowing from Tomorrow's egg.

## London Company

Gentlemen in good lace and brocade,
Carpenters and other artisans,

Sad-suited merchants, seafarers, adventurers whose corselets
Had mirrored fields and skies of a dozen countries,

We were all sorts—ships' companies, no more,
And every ship is like a little world.

What had we to do with each other, or with those deserts?
Each had his own hope, or his own despair,

And each his own America, till at last we saw it,
Like Atlantis risen foaming out of the sea,

Fateful as a prophecy fulfilled,
Unknown as the still world after death.

Some sailed back, quickly enough; some died; the rest of us
Remained; endured; what bound us?

Remember, it was an alien continent,
Its clouds and its forests ringing with strange birds,

Its meadows brimming with nameless flowers, its streams
Born in darkness, amid secret hills;

Who can take joy in the flowering of a foreign spring?
And yet, a solemn mystery was accomplished:

The wilderness fruits we ate and made one with our bodies,
We exchanged our breath for that untasted air.

Our dead we laid in the wild earth, the twain dusts easily mingling;
Then this was no more an alien land.

Each of us had his will, or did not have it,
Made his fortune or did not, and no matter,

But men in blindness build, like coral, ignorant
Of their own building; greatness all unguessed

Possesses them and blesses them, builds union
In what was most diverse; so with us,

Most fortunate at last in the hardest of our fortunes,
One with the earth we earned; a nation our monument.

## The Minstrels Rebuked

Hang up the ancestral harp, and put away
The antique flute; the old minstrelsy is finished.
No more of courtly or of learned themes;
The great courts all have fallen; what's learning worth
When he who runs may write as well as read?
It is proclaimed that in all gardens now
The rose shall be no better than the weed;
A brazen cock has cried up a new day,
Driven out the nightingale, and hailed the jay.

What folly made you master the old skill?
Who knows the master from the apprentice now?
How could the flute's clear discourse and the lyre's
Eloquence be heard above this din?
Pack up such toys, I say; if play you will,
Play the music that our age requires,
Practice to split the ear with a bawling horn,
Make mad bombardments on the kettledrum,
Go battering on any empty tin.

## Punch and Judy Songs

**BUTCHER**

A butcher has to handle flesh,
That cannot be denied;
Why not that dainty morsel?
That's what I thought, and died.

**BAKER**

That oven was hot as hot,
With nothing at all inside;
Why should he grudge my little loaf?
That's what I thought, and died.

**CANDLESTICK-MAKER**

Although I dealt in candlesticks,
A certain candle was my pride;
Why not that fancy socket for it?
That's what I thought, and died.

**JUDY**

His hate was generous as love,
I had the costliest gems to wear;
What jewel's more costly than a tear?

Passion I had abundance of,
Passion that pierced me to the marrow;
What passion runs more deep than sorrow?

**PUNCH**

A woman on her back is good,
Better is a woman on her knees;
Change all your sweetly simpering loves
To spitting, clawing enemies:

I slept with her three thousand nights,
Had no such pleasure from her bed,
No such shuddering ecstasy,
As on the night I choked her dead.

HANGMAN

Silence is the most delicate music,
Though difficult to hear;
None dance so delicately
As hanged men dancing upon air.

Leap and bow and swing, my pretty,
There's nothing daintier anywhere;
None dance so delicately
As hanged men dancing upon air.

## Preview, Informal

Look. Look. A jungle forest, sun-shot, branch-
Brown, leaf-green. Dropping down
From branch to branch a randy band of scarlet
Monkeys, snowy-ruffed, black-velvet-masked,
Ruffle all the hanging strings of blooms
And falls of bell-flowers, yet do not startle
The haughty birds displayed here: macaws, toucans,
Crested parakeets whose sultry fans
Beat back the heat. The birds perch or fly,
But do not snap the dragonflies that strike
Like lightnings down the sun-drift. Look, look! Rippling
Coil on figured coil a giant serpent
Terrifies nothing, neither bird nor monkey.
The serpent yawns and shows a stripèd maw,
The birds swing on, turning indifferent eyes,
The monkeys leap and dangle. Look! through the bamboo-grass
Magnificent, lion-colored, kingly-curled,
A lion pads; behind him steps a deer.
The lion turns and roars one golden roar
And then lies down; the deer beds down beside,
Accomplishing, almost, the prophecy.
No blood has ever brightened the dark ground.
The jungle rings incessantly with cries
Yet these are not of agony or joy
But music simply, meaningless as the music
Of the stream wandering, tinkling as if in memory
Of dews and rains in caves and dells deep underground.
Confess this world is excellent and fair.
You are present in imagination only,
For else you could not see it; this is a world
Purified, perfected; an on-Second-Thought-and-
Better-Thought Creation; made after yours,

The one great Error rectified. Do you understand?—
Birds, beasts, insects, flowers, trees, are all
Automata; yes, yes, mechanical toys.
Come, come—was life so valuable, after all?
I especially like that lion-colored lion.

# For the Demolition of a Theater

The player was neither king nor clown;
Of tragedy or comedy,
Truth is the last catastrophe.

Paper castles, too, fall down;
Spider and mouse have always known
A false world ends in real debris.

This is the scene none cared to see,
True autumn in the plaster tree.
Walk the mouldering stage, alone,

Put on the dimmed and battered crown,
Mount the cobwebbed cardboard throne,
Command the ruinous painted sea;

O Prince of dreams, mock-Majesty,
Nothing stays the ruinous sea;
Even the painted waves roll on,

Even the dreamt kingdoms drown.

## A Valentine for Marianne Moore

The hardest thing to imagine is
The fact perfectly seen. Tannhäuser's miracle
Repeated, certainly; the blossoming
Pilgrim's-staff, thought dead wood. Anyone sees
The wintry stick; a few can fancy flowers
And are called poets; the truly rare
Eye sees what is really there:
The dry stick shaken with implicit spring,

Imagination
More precise than sensation
Because it is governed by an intellect
More precise than either. Pleasure, said Aristotle,
Is perfect when the perfect organ finds
Its worthiest object; pleasure then
Perfects the perfected activity
As youth is perfected by the bloom of youth.
This is your perfection, Madam; there is
Nothing more beautiful than perfect truth

Except the mind that sees it. Poetry, to be
Poetry truly, must be more than poetry; in perfection
It is never fiction,
It never falsifies. Detestable the eloquence
That must turn every pebble to a jewel
To make it a fit subject; yes, and hateful
The raging of a false poetic fire,
The bellows working audibly; but Plato
Would have loved your poems; would have wondered, too, to see
Poems ordered like his Perfect State.

True beauty is most truly praised
By the glass which is most true.

Madam, this glass is mine,
The loveliness within is you.
Accept this for your valentine.
It has my heart's shape, and no more;
I scorn to dress it with the common lace;
Let it have no grace but your grace.

# Mobile by Calder

A shoal of burnished fish
Suspended, feeding; sunset boats
Gently rocking, in harbor; perhaps a shower
Of falling autumn leaves that never fall;
Anything at all,
So that we understand invisible poise
Translated to visible balance,
Stillness to motion:

More than anything, like a new universe:
How pleasant that a man can make his own universe,
Where all the worlds are turning metal vanes,
And One does not always equal One,
One may equal Five or Ten or Twenty;
How clever an artist, to know that motion,
All motion, implies a point of poise,
All fictions turn upon a point of truth;

And to prove once more, by a new universe, more clearly seen,
That things, whatever they are, propose a principle
Without which they could not be, or be as they are,
And to say, thus, what ships, stars, leaves,
Fish,
And other things have been saying a long time,
Though until now, until now, we did not hear.

# The Last Entries in the Journal

*"To leave quietly,
as one leaves a movie,
careful not to disturb anyone."*

## I

The forests rusted, and released their leaves,
And the wind took the leaves. He said: Let the wind take them.
I have written all my wisdom upon all the leaves,
Let the wind take them, not to publish abroad,
But simply to remove, as valueless
Relics of a worthless season ended.
I will start anew, I will write a newer wisdom.
Waking that night, he woke to the cold clouds'
Silent provision: a fresh page of snow.
But that lay blank until the arbutus wrote
What it had written many times before.

## II

Certainly it is the self makes all the difference:
The martyr suffers ecstasy at the stake;
The voluptuary, torment in his pleasures.

I loathe my image in the midnight mirror,
Seeing tomorrow's man I made today.

## III

The function of the eye is not to ache,
Only to see; what pain it suffers then
Is but the consequence of that sensitivity
Whereby the eye is eye and apt to see.
I infer, thus, that the great design is good,
And pain and evil are mere accidents.
Where did I get such wisdom? From long study,

Study of the scriptures of my wounds.
What have the roses written on my wall?

My soul, if every wound became a rose—

## IV

Problem: to hear the battering storm as music,
But never, drunk with harmony, be deaf
To all the dissonances compounding harmony.
Problem: after swimming all the oceans,
Not to drown within this drop of dew.
Memo: not to choke on my own breath.

## V

Dwelling amid mountains
Zarathustra conceived the Superman.
This is what comes of
Dwelling amid mountains.

## VI

Let me hear no more of the far-sighted man.
The starbeam travelled many million miles
And Simpleton, because he saw the star,
Thought he could see those many million miles.
Far sight and near sight
See only what impinges on the eye.

## VII

We must go beyond the evidence; certainly Reason
Can be confined too narrowly to its data:
This fellow, picking over mammoth's bones,
Concludes that skeletons once walked the earth.

## VIII

How bitterly the Snowman hates
Even the winter sun.
His element is moonlit air, the heatless moon
Turns him to diamond. Diamond is not sun,
Snow is not diamond; we must have sun.

## IX

Beware the eye of the geometer,
Where shaped and colored world is diagram.
Beware that eerie algebraic brain
Where heaven and earth are both replaced by numbers.
Remember, the whole miserable affair
Began by inventing zero and negative numbers.
Beware what gives an entity to nullity,
Gives quantity to what lacks quantity,
And turns the concrete into the abstract.
Observe these fruits, piled on a silver plate.
There is the problem; let our reasoning not lose sight of them.

## X

"Climbing out of a pit is far, far harder
Than climbing a mountain. But no one, no one applauds."

## XI

Play that wild delicate Prelude, as if the wind
Swept the glimmering harpstrings of the rain.
The man who wrote it had a broken heart:
Beauty alone survives, of all his sorrows.

## XII

The crows' harsh cries prelude autumnal music
And find in that their concord. Discord is meaningless

Except as establishing the principle
Of harmonies to be. Pain, too, is meaningless
Save as preluding peace; and suffering
Itself ennobles no one; it degrades,
Unless it is resolved at last to joy.

## XIII

As if all sufferance
Were like the sufferance of love.
The torn hind amorous
Of the rending lion,
All her terror and pain
Frenzy of amorous delight,
As if fang and claw but free
Her from her unendurable ecstasy.

## XIV

*Agitato doppio movimento;*
The piano raging in the twilight room,
The wind raging through the ruined wood,
The sea raging at its barriers. Rage on,
Strike the great chord like clashing shields, the chord
That brings the brazen towers clanging down,
And last, the chord that cleaves the universe.
You shall not find your resolution so;
All chords resolve on the one chord of silence.

## XV

Autumn again; again and yet again.
Am I for this, then? To count seasons out?
I thought, once, I should name the secret names
Of all that is, and keep all being safe,
Locked in the little thunders of the tongue.

## XVI

For this, that history of torment? Soul's-rape of birth,
Agony and shame of growth?

                              Ship-wrecked by my lusts,
Cast up, panting, on white shores of flesh?
—That's my blood on the world, I have trailed it everywhere,
You may read my whole history in it. Let me put on my mask;
Ugly, perhaps; but I can't speak truth without it.

## XVII

Peace, poor soul; peace, peace, for God's sake, peace;
This is your world, and you were made for it;
Why should the dung-beetle quarrel with the dung?

## XVIII

Well: the fiddle is broken; in its whole career
It gave out only a single perfect tone.
For this a tree was felled, and a cat died.
The tone had nothing to do with cat and tree.

## XIX

Alas, cried Adam from his ancient grave,
How brief a time Death wears our human form
And how long afterwards he wears his own.

## XX

The last slow-gathering spasm; as if a clock
Strained and strained to strike; and could not strike.

## XXI

"How cruel of the wolf, to kill the deer,"
The child cries out; the grown man, silent, knows
The wolf that kills the deer is merciful:
Without the wolf that kills, all deer would die.

## XXII

The arctic cold sets in; by ancient instinct
Most birds have fled; the rest are housed or shielded,
Caribou and moose have stamped their yards,
The bears are lodged, beast after beast lies snug,
Sheltered from ice and snow by ice and snow.
Beneath thick ice the fish are safe.—Merciful!
More than merciful; a thread of mercy
Woven through creation; older than creation.
For the instinct precedes the peril; thus,
The mercy was before the storm was made.

## XXIII

To be glad that good exists, though you have no benefit;
Caught in the whirlpool, sinking in quicksand, to rejoice
That some walk safely; at the freezing Pole
To hail the sun that warms world after world
But sends with all its rays no ray for you.

## XXIV

Man is not necessary to the earth;
Life, even, is not; nothing is really needful
But Earth itself, revolving in its orbit
As counterweight to other moving spheres,
That they may move and shine. Move, then, and shine;
Nothing but motion, perhaps, yet in that motion
There is perpetual equilibrium
Of all the flying elements of motion.
This, it may be, is the only order,
And this the only peace that you may know.
Nevertheless there are, then, order and peace.

## XXV

Arise and look, the dream said; it is there.
And dreaming still, he rose and went outdoors.
All the air glistened with stars and snow:

The farthest star shot down a ray and struck
The nearest snow-flake, that itself a star,
And at its center kindled a new star
That lived just long enough to flash one ray
Back to the farthest star. There you have it:
Things with no connection, the immense, the minute,
The most perduring, the most transitory,
Somehow connected, across unimaginable gulfs.

# PART V

# Ice-Skaters

Snow-hills all about,
And snowy woods; and snow
Falling: a full moon's out;

The river's frozen; across
Its avenue of ice
Vivid skaters swirl

In the cold, in the moon's light.
Look, look: the young, the old,
Set moving by delight.

—The whole town's on the ice!
Whirling in a gay
Preposterous ballet.

Look, the strides, the glides,
Cossack-leaps, dervish-twirls,
Clown-tumblings, clown-falls!

Racers, rapt in speed
As in an ecstasy,
Swerving in a flash of sleet;

Lovers, hand in hand,
Enchanted by their own
Music without sound,

And the older pairs,
A little clumsy now,
But merry as waltzing bears,

And children, intently
Scuffing foot by foot,
Stiffly rocking in and out,

All intricately winding in a Christmas-colored maze
With Lord, what a racket! till the hills
Go wild with echoes, bellow like mad bulls

And in the dark ravines
Beneath the crystal floor
Fish quiver, and wave their fins.

The town clock chimes the hour
Unheeded: let it chime,
Time has lost its power.

What monkey-shines, what fun!
Flesh is no burden now,
It never lay so lightly on the bone.

The body too can be
Spirit, when set free
By pure delight of motion

Without destination;
Shows its own fantasy,
Wit, and imagination.

Is this the being Lear could call
A poor, bare,
Forked animal?

Strike that out; say this,
That in a harsh season,
Above a dark abyss,

The mortal creature
Rejoiced in its own nature;
Revelled, itself the reason.

—Why, life's a carnival! Snow
Falls like confetti now;
The moon, in comic mood,

Turns to a grotesque
Snowball; hides in cloud;
Comes back in a clown's mask.

The skaters swirl and swirl;
All their motions cry
It is joy, sheer joy,

That makes the atoms dance
And wings the flying stars
And speeds the sun upon his golden course.

# *Mirror*

The gown falls fold on fold.
Sway in those burnished coils,
Lift your delicate head,
Lean to your mirror, stare
Into those brilliant eyes
Till they grow dark and bleak.
This is not vanity,
Disliking what you see;
Gaze on: you too surmise
The bitter secret there.
Press your hand to your breast,
You too are appalled:
What you thought your love
Was nothing but the cold,
The ravaging inner cold,
That drives the wilderness snake
Into the woodsman's bed.

# Taxco

A mountain town, on mountains among mountains,
A town of balconies opening to the sun,
White villas, white arcades and colonnades,
Rouge roofs like terraces of wavy tile,
All half-engulfed in fronds and flowering trees.
Over the laurels in the little square
A rose cathedral lifts its twin bell-towers,
Swings bells of weathered bronze, intones, intones.

Stone the color of an album-rose
Shapes, in its fantasies, crossed papal keys,
Dreams awhile of John baptising Christ,
Sets spirals on pilasters to ascend
Through cherubs, anthemia, and evangelists
To airy belfries where grave angels gaze.
At last both faith and science crown the whole:
The cross stands paramount with the lightning-rod.

Those unhelped by either god must cower,
Crouch at the door, and beg for copper coins:
The crone, the child who carries in her shawl
A dying baby smaller than a doll,
The drunken paralytic, the plump man
Who pleads while tossing off an orangeade.
We endow them all, beholding in their eyes
The ancient sorrowing eyes that saw Cortéz.

The town ascends with the steep mountain-sides;
We climb and climb, up flint and basalt, stones
Sharp and precipitous, cobbles keenly set,
Streets that are stairs, or stony beds of brooks.
Traffic like a mysterious Exodus

Winds all about us—burros, buses, cars,
Goats, pigs, horsemen, women wearing hens,
Small boys in basket-hats piled high with bread.

Every alcove is a silver shop;
Silver glistens in a thousand shapes
As if a humbler Midas wandering here
Had turned to silver all his hands could touch.
In the soft moon-like sheen that silver sheds
Two men are playing chess, and the great board
Is silver and ebony, the chessmen are
Images of silver and ruddy gold.

—A page from some fable of emperors at play,
Dreamed by the poor to ease their poverty;
But at our elbows are the poor themselves,
Carrying colored paper bound on sticks
—The flowers of the poor, in a land of flowers.
After them comes the gauze-bound coffin, borne
By men who bear a heavier burden still.
All drag heavy shadows down the hill.

The buzzards hunching, shawled in their great wings,
In the fringed jacarandas at high noon
Have deep thoughts, doubtless, justifying death.
These sable scholars have a *parti pris*,
Yet here, on the holy Festival of the Dead,
Merry children munch on sugar skulls,
Crunch candy bones, discovering death is sweet.
Is death an ending? Toys deck children's graves.

Mexican earth—blood-red, blood-black, bone-yellow,
Bone-gray, skull-white—recounts mortality,
But fires wild blooms, like rockets, at the sun.

There are other enigmas: we trouble an old bell
Rusting above a door of battered boards,
Enter to tame jungles sheltering
A Roman villa, and imperial lawns,
And all the courtliness of old Roman Spain.

At dusk, over daiquiris, in the high hotel,
We ponder a little on the world we saw;
Fail, as usual, at that strange charade.
What is Taxco? What is Mexico?
Clouds drift beneath us, and a giant palm
Rattles its leaves in chilly mountain air,
The dogs begin to bark, a far cock crows;
Suddenly the whole town has turned to stars,

Keeps star-like silence, till a burro's bray
Rasps like a rusty pump in a dry well.
That inarticulate cry is eloquent
For all those comfortless under the ancient moon,
Those whom no chance or change can benefit.
And now the marimbas and the mandolins
Ring out, the dissonant bells begin their din,
—All voices crying, *I am Mexico:*

None is, although all are. Perhaps the land
Has its true image in some silent thing.
The moon illumines mountains and mountainous cloud,
And all the forests stand in silent light,
But for some cloud-like reason I recall
A woman at prayer before a crucifix.
The world, I reflect, is merely what it means,
Remembering the passion in that wrinkled face

Though cross and Christ were only woven straw.

# The Green Christmas

Christmas came the twelfth of May.
The children trooping down the walk
Saw reindeer and sleigh on the green lawn
And strung lights winking, oddly wan
In the bright middle of the day.
They saw the wreath on the front door;
Confused but festive, pushed to see
In one sunny upstairs room
A snowman with hat, scarf, and broom,
And a dazzling Christmas tree.

Despite the candy and the toys
They found that Christmas was less fun
Somehow, on the twelfth of May;
An hour or so, and they were gone.
The Wilsons, though, were fiercely gay
A little longer; gay until
Suddenly man and wife were still;
She, for some strange woman's-reason,
Straightening the room, while he
Gazed at the young and fragrant tree,

It, too, struck down in its green season,
And yet, he thought, less wantonly.

## A Dream for a Sad Lady

Troubled lady, sleep.
Sleep turns all to dream,
Time turns every woe
To legend or song at last.
Sleep, and sleeping, dream
Today was long ago:

Dream of an age past:
Music wafts over the waters,
In a cloud-mirroring sea
Drifts a delicate ship.
Beneath a light canopy
A moon-pale Empress dreams:
You are the dream she dreams.
At her feet a slave
Holds some harp-like instrument, sings
Of legendary things
To the singing strings:
It is your grief she sings.

# The Attack on the Jungle Train

"Nothing has ever happened to this train."

"Look, with hearts and diamonds—a safe journey,
  Lots of money! Now stop worrying."

"I always just remember, *God is Love*."

"They're only—well, just *bandits*—aren't they?"

"With five cars full of soldiers right behind us?"

The heat bore down and silenced them at last.
Hours of baked and faded plains; then mountains,
Mountains and mountains, with one particular mountain
Of a peculiar and unpleasant shape
That kept on turning up, to right, to left,
Before, behind; not to be shaken off.
At last they escaped it, shooting a wild curve
Where trees sprang up from ambush, and closed round.
Then they were in an interminable tunnel.
It was cooler now; sweaty clothes grew chill.

"I thought this thing ran mostly through a jungle."

"We're *in* the jungle, fella!"

                    Taylor stared.
Where were the hanging fronds, the fountaining ferns,
The cliffs of leaves and waterfalls of flowers?
He saw what might have been a twilight shipyard,
Poles, immense masts, standing in brown gloom,
Draped anyhow with cables and fouled cordage.

"You a Nature-lover? Well—that's Nature;
   And every single bit of it out there
   Loves you too, as food or fertilizer,
   Though some of it would rather have manure.
   Don't ask *it* questions—it might answer you."

Taylor said nothing. The difficulty was
He had to have one answer, just to live.
The man behind them tapped him on the shoulder:
"They say that every sleeper in this stretch
Cost one workman. Still—the track got built.
Think what that means!"

                          Abruptly the train ran
Into a blazing fire; that was a clearing,
A clearing all hot rocks; as suddenly
They seemed to crash head-on into the sun,
Lumber came in and tumbled down the aisle.

Some lunatic was capering in a cloud
—It was escaping steam—till he collapsed
As if worn out.
                     Beside a burning car
Ragged men were stirring bundled rags
With, it seemed, sticks.
                               Someone shook him—"Taylor!
Answer me—can you hear me? We've got to run,
They're bayoneting the survivors! *Taylor?*

He could not move. The voice went off at last.

He lay and waited for the bayonet,
And had his vision. Butterflies—brilliant, undisturbed
Butterflies weaving in a ritual dance
Over a pool of blood; a kind of emblem
Of something that undoubtedly existed,
But as rapt in its own activity, unconcerned
With human good or evil; even, perhaps,
Ignorant that humankind had come to be;
Seeing, perhaps, no difference between
A galaxy and the smallest grain of sand.

## At a Military Ceremony

Praise the soldier innocent as his rifle,
Praise him in the splendor of his wounds
More terrible than Sebastian's or Christ's:

Say that flower-like from his blood in the fiery wastes
Tall cities spring, where lights hang thick as dews,
And peace, like perfume from a saint's tomb, wells;

The altar is painful enough, may the victim perish
Ignorant that his gods are sticks and stones
And that this death is death, like any other.

## Old Story New Hero

The Giant fell sprawling on his back,
Crushing the ancient oaks like grass:
The wild blood roaring from his wound
Cascaded down the mountain-pass;

The Dragon thrashed, and rolled his coils,
Strong in the agonies of death;
His tail in spasm scourged the flames
Of forests blazing with his breath;

And shuddering, the Magician's Tower
Ground stone on stone, and cracked, and broke,
All its stampeding horrors now
Streaming out of it like smoke;

Sir Hero knelt by the mountain lake
Dark with reflected balsam and pine,
Took off his helm, and saw his face
Stamped with defeat in every line.

# Chess-Game

My enemy and I are playing chess,
Trapped by an idiot's-trick of circumstance,
A rainy week-end, and a woman's whim.
Civilization effects this, at least,
That face to face in rigid courtesy
We sit like friends, and share a narrow board:
Two who can barely breathe in the same world.

What mends the manners need not mend the man.
To be unmended is to reënact,
Ghost-like, old wickedness; and so we do:
Reckless as emperors, we sacrifice
Pawns ignorant as peasants why they die.
Now I trick him with a wooden horse,
His castle falls as bitterly as Troy.

What's strong as hatred? Joy has no such glee,
Greed is less eager, love less intimate.
Locked in an intricate interplay as fierce
And delicate as the tact of swords, we know
Each other to the soul—can love do that?—
Feel our own blows, exchange identities;
Becoming each other, remain enemies.

I move, and nearly pinch my pawn in half,
His nostrils sharpen as he shifts his queen.
Knight, castle, king—all ancient symbols, almost
Meaningless now, powerless in themselves,
But potent still with powers we still confer.
What if we should deny them?—We do not;
Cling to our antique world, four-cornered, flat;

And hosts identical in all but hue
Make hue their quarrel, having nothing else,
The godless priests pursue their bias still,
The lightless uninhabitable towers
Move from their stations, and four horsemen ride
Till all are swept away, to leave behind
Empty spaces, blackened, or stained red.

# Palindrome

The sun rose in the west:
The cities shrank to stones.
A wilderness sprang up
Where rivers ran reversed.
Empires declined
To their origins.
Though bone and dust of bone
Put on flesh and walked,
Though all the starved grew poor'
Though folly of crusades
Lacked folly of the cross,
Nothing, nothing was changed,
All was as before:
Madness and death
And poverty and war.
All was as before,
Only more meaningless.

## Directions to the Armorer

All right, armorer,
Make me a sword—
Not too sharp,
A bit hard to draw,
And of cardboard, preferably.
On second thought, stick
An eraser on the handle.
Somehow I always
Clobber the wrong guy.

Make me a shield with
Easy-to-change
Insignia. I'm often
A little vague
As to which side I'm on,
What battle I'm in.
And listen, make it
A trifle flimsy,
Not too hard to pierce.
I'm not absolutely sure
I want to win.

Make the armor itself
As tough as possible,
But on a reverse
Principle: don't
Worry about its
Saving my hide;
Just fix it to give me
Some sort of protection—
Any sort of protection—
From a possible enemy
Inside.

# The Side of the Bread

At first I think he's loco, he looks so funny-like,
Pale, and his eyes hot, breathing like he was shivering.
"Come here," he says. "What do you think of that?"
It was the biggest, fattest sow I ever saw.
"What in heck did you do—cross a boar with a whale?"
"That ain't nothing," he says. "Take a look at this."
It was a farmer's nightmare—a wheatfield in a pot,
A hundred big ears on one stalk of corn,
And a big bean-plant fit to scare the sweat off you.
Jack and his Beanstalk wasn't in the running;
You could see that this thing meant to poke through clouds.
"Believe it or not, I planted that last week."
He was shaking like a leaf, and so was I.
"I been experimenting, I found something,
I wasn't even looking for it."
                              "Listen," I says,
"You sell me some of that whatever-it-is,
We'll both make millions."
                              "We won't make nothing," he says,
And then I think he's really going crazy.
He started hollering like a jackleg preacher
Anybody could make it anywhere out of anything
And he was going to tell them how to do it
And crops like that would wipe out deserts and jungles,
Nobody'd be hungry, nobody'd be poor,
Might be no more wars even, leastways over crops and land,
That kind of talk.
                    I tried to reason with him
We'd all be ruined in a ruined market
With every tailor farming in his thimble
And prize stock begging at a cent a head,

He wouldn't listen.
                    "All that don't signify.
I'm going to phone right now and tell the *Gazette*,
In an hour everybody in the States,
In a day or two everybody in the world,
Even the Chinks and Russians, 'll know about it."

"If that's what you want," I says, and look around.
There was nothing handy but a chunk of rock,
So I grab that. It took me a long time.

I didn't want no murder charge or nothing,
I got the neighbors together, told them the facts,
Backed up my story with the sow and plants.
They knew which side their bread was buttered on,
Nobody blamed me; we all just set to looking
To find that stuff or his, or else a formula,
Ripped the place apart, dug all over it,
Never found nothing.
                    It was a damn shame.
Stuff like that, a fella'd plant a seed
And have to run like he lit dynamite
Or a whole wheatfield'd explode right in his face.
Beans like that would have eat up any bugs or bacteria.
No hail wouldn't hurt that corn; even hail like baseballs,
You could just of took one of them cornstalks,
Batted the whole shebang back where it came from.
Too bad, all right.
                    Sure would of come in handy
Couple years later—I mean when we had that blight,
And lost all the livestock, and even the locusts starved.

# The Impersonation

Returning from the diner you had the first inkling
Of the plot against you: a man was in your seat,
Dressed exactly like you; in fact, your double.
It was sheer luck that you managed to hide
Before the others came down the aisle, searching for you
With evident intentions; sheer luck, too,
That you found the wherewithal for a disguise
So that you could safely ride out the rest of the journey,
In full view, by a window, as if simply watching
The short twilight of the winter day,
The dripping towns, the lights of scattered farms.
When at last out of the long tunnel of night
The train ran into the great bright terminus,
You watched "yourself" descend, to be greeted eagerly
By your wife and children; could you have protested?
Perhaps, perhaps; but you saw who was drawing near you,
And fled, as you had to; a week later, you were stumbling
Through thick woods, under a lowering sky,
Disturbing snow-laden brambles, dislodging wreaths of snow,
With them a step behind you; they nearly had you, later,
On that knuckle of rock by the sullen coiling river.
It was touch and go, too, in the sodden flats
With the salt-like snow hissing down in the sear grasses
And strings of wild swans flying over; well, well—
Why go through the whole story? Suffice it to say
You were hunted out of your life for years and years
And meanwhile your life was lived by someone else
And when at last you managed to return
You found yourself within a cemetery
Where mourners watched a coffin being lowered.
There, in the box, you were; yourself at last.
And you think all this unusual? My poor friend!
Millions, millions, millions live and die so.

## Plaza México

At half past four a trumpet stills the crowd.
A man in the court-dress of Cervantes' day
Rides out upon a daintily-stepping bay,
Lifts his hat before the President's box,
Bows on his curtseying horse, catches the ribboned
Keys to the toril locks,
Bows, withdraws.
                Band-music erupts,
A tiny army makes its brief parade:
The matadors in armor of brocade,
The tinsel pawns, the basin-helmeted
Quixotes upon quilted jades;
Last, a jingling team of mules.

The bull sweeps the ring free
Of every brilliant enemy;
Head high, sharp-horned as the moon,
Claims this new dominion as his own.
Now all that the posters promised comes to be:

Bull-lunges, cape-work, horses overthrown,
Violence and serenity, until
In the strange stillness of the thousands still
Swordsman and bull confront each other, stand
Alone upon the great red disk of sand.

The bull
Broods in his raying spears;
Tail up, charges; charges once again;
Ponders, at last in doubt;
Then, the sword-hilt plain
Amid the barbs, the blood,

Turns away, moves to the barriers;
There
Beds down; at the knife-blow, rolls
Over, legs in air.
The mules jingle in and jingle out
And the crowd stirs,
The crowd stirs, suddenly
Relieved that, after all,
It has not seen what it half hoped to see.

# Conversation between a Mirror and the Sea

**THE SEA**

For all my depth, my surface is a mirror.

**THE MIRROR**

I am a surface, I reflect a depth.

# Exposition of the Quarrel of the Birds

The quarrel is between
Those who must have meaning in the music
And those who find the meaning *in* the music
And those who would prefer what meanings mean
(And those who just like music, anyway);

It is between
Those who would say the water-drop and those
Who hold that one who says the water-drop
Can say no more than water-drops can say
(And those who would say clouds, or leaves, or stones);

Between
Those who think the note must be prolonged
And those who think it cannot and it must not,
Between those who like a statement and those who prefer
The delicate inflections of interrogation.

The quarrel is between
Those who insist that the true note is sounded
Aloft, only, as from high heaven,
And those who think it can be uttered only
Close to the earth, from grass or ditch or furrow

And between
Those who find the music in the music
And those who find the music in the silence
After, or before; and those who find
The music in what silence and song imply.

Between those who think the barkings of the crow
Can never be beautiful as the syllables of the thrush
And those who call the crow's voice beautiful
Because of its rough wit, and because it suits the crow
(And that, *too*, suits the crow!) Also between

Those who grieve that the cry of the eagle grows rarer and rarer
And those who never liked eagles or eagle-music;
Between those who hold that the mockingbird
Has no voice of its own, and those who observe
That no other bird has the voice of the mockingbird;

The quarrel is between
Birds, is all bickerings of song-birds on a summer morning,
Voices cast this way or that, from contrary directions,
From cloud, from forest-deep, meadow, roadside or brookside,
But all musical, and in very quarrel, in very dissonance

Harmonious, making up a morning's music,
All together weaving a summer morning,
Making in music an image of the morning
So that we cannot think that morning apart from its music.

(There are also the frogs, and the bugs; and *they* hold that—)

# The Argument about the Decoration of the Punch Table

HE:

Good heavens, woman! Crystal,
Ice-crystal, and ice-blue
At this time of the year!
Frosty silver, too,
A cloth like Arctic snows,
And that monstrous icicle,
That stalactite chandelier!
Why, it's the Snow King's house!
No one will venture here
But explorers and Eskimos,
And they will freeze to the soul;
Blizzards will swirl and howl
Through all the rooms, the table
Will glare like the North Pole.

Don't go to the other extreme:
I won't have a tropic isle,
All frond and fern and vine,
Bunched bananas and grapes
Glimmering in musky gloom.
Bangled women will slink
Like cannibals everywhere;
The men will turn into apes
Swinging from bough to bough,
And chase them through every room;
Or else the lot will sink
Into a languid, slow,
Lotus-Eater's dream
And never want to go home.
We've asked them in for a drink;
Do you want them to winter here?

Trim it with balsam and pine
That speak of winters withstood;
Leaves, and the winter berry
That can light up a dark wood;
All, say, in the design
Of a hunter's lean-to, good
From an hour's relief from the storm,
An hour for friends to be warm
And so be friendly and merry,
An hour when the wind cannot find them.
Yes—leaves, boughs, then
Silver enough to remind them
Of all that silver outside,
Of the cold they have braved and beaten.
Let them go—
Having drunk, having eaten—
Braced to brave it again.

SHE:

No.

# Exhibition of Modern Art

### 1

Luminous airy carrousel,
Light thoughts like children ride your round.

### 2

The great blood-lit vein-branching tree
Is full of leaves and babes unborn:
Through all those centuries of storm
Humanity was a still tree.

### 3

Such wintry silences could come
Only from green violins.
Or violinists with green skins.

### 4

Is the universe, as this painter says,
Prisms intersecting prisms?
No, says this, it is opaque
And shines like new linoleum.

### 5

The girl with orange hair complains
(One of her eyes is blue, the other brown)
Because the hair of the painted girl is green.

### 6

Two spoons,
Spooning. Note that each mirrors the other,
So that what each sees, if it sees—
Let us leave, we might embarrass them.

### 7

Only, perhaps,
A moment of unrecapturable surprise
As when a child first finds
Echo speaks his language, too.

### 8

"Nothing looks like that! What's it called?"
"*Nothing*."

### 9

I have seen many humming-birds but
Now I have seen this (which does not depict a humming-bird)
At last I know what a humming-bird looks like.

### 10

The lady next to me likes pictures of flowers
But this is how flowers look to a fish.
Yet the retired boxer understands:
"That's just the way it is when you're knocked out."

### 11

Paint black on black on black on black on black?
Are these the landscapes that a blindman sees,
Or theorems of immortality?

### 12

O cold construction, what strict rigors wrought
Such chill constriction, geometric spasm?
O incommunicable passion felt
Only by the disconnected refrigerator,
Let me have life and violence: the colors
When a volcano explodes like a curse.

### 13

"Why do I always find myself standing
  On tip-toe before this picture?"
"This one will set you back on your heels."

### 14

These levitations you may wonder at
Who never saw Chagall drift through a door.

### 15

"Well—a rain-forest at night
  All lit up with fire-flies."
"No—
  It says, *Snow*."

### 16

Pure colors storming in pellucid wind,
Cleanse my vision: it is like dirty ice
Reflecting nothing.

### 17

"They say that it's a portrait of his mistress."
"I'd throw her over for the Brooklyn Bridge."

### 18

Look how this lonely piece of metal yearns
For this other; is metal also not exempt?

### 19

Yes, it can look like that,
It doesn't matter what.
Terror and despair
Have their own special air.
Everything looks like that
In the colors of despair.

### 20

*Argument from Design:*
Only I can't find
The design.

### 21

"What is beauty, saith my sufferings, then?"
"Beauty is its own excuse for being."
"Beauty is in the eye of the beholder."
"Look at my ball," said the beetle, "isn't it beautiful?"

### 22

See: children
Find all this no stranger than the world.

### 23

We hear in Time, we see in Space.
Break, Time, that we may hear.
Break, Space, that we may see.
"Else a great prince in prison lies."
The prisoner of sense is not
Imprisoned when the sense is not.

Was I not made insensate then
By very action of the sense
When all the while the roses sang,
The nightingales perfumed the night?

# A Toast

I praise the weaknesses
That make us fellows;
Fine faults, that keep us kin.

Great virtue brings esteem; great vice, disdain.
Both estrange; yet why should mortal men
Be, like gods and demons, set apart?

Far better, far, that sharing a small sin
We hear the beat of the one animal heart,
Feel with one nerve, and live in the same skin.

Fellows in fault, it is to be at once
Forgiving and forgiven makes us one:
It is our common fault that binds us kin.

To that implacable Angel, the stern Scribe
Of heaven or of our consciences, I wish
Short memory, bad ink, a sputtering pen:

Our faults, our common faults, have kept us kin.

# The Graveyard by the Sea

FROM THE FRENCH OF PAUL VALÉRY

*Do not, beloved Soul, strive after immortal life,*
*but rather pursue practicable things.*

PINDAR, Pythian Ode III

This quiet roof, where doves are wandering,
Trembles between the pines, between the tombs;
Noon, the just Noon, stills with even fires
The sea, the sea, forevermore renewed.
What recompense to follow on a thought:
A long gaze upon the calm of gods!

What pure work of keen lightnings here consumes
Many a diamond of imperceptible foam,
And what a peace, as of itself conceived!
When a sun reposes over the abyss,
Pure effects of an eternal cause,
Time sparkles, and the Dream becomes the knowing.

Firm treasure, simple temple to Minerva,
Mass of calm, and visible reserve,
Arrogant-browed water, Eye that holds
So much sleep beneath a veil of flame,
O my silence! Edifice in the soul,
But Roof of gold, the myriad-tiled top.

Temple of Time, whose history is a sigh,
To this pure point I climb, and wont myself,
Ringed all around by my own seaward gaze;
And, like my ultimate offering to the gods,
The radiance, serenely sparkling, sows
Upon the height a sovereign disdain.

As fruit in its enjoyment melts away,
Altering its absence to delight
Within a mouth where its form perishes,
I breathe, here, the smoke that I shall be,
And the sky sings to the soul consumed
The alteration of the murmurous shores.

Bright sky, true sky, witness my altering!
After such haughtiness, after so much strange
Indolence, but filled with power still,
I give myself over to this brilliant space.
Over the houses of the dead my shadow
Moves, subduing me to its frail motion.

My soul exposed to torches of the solstice,
I sustain you, admirable justice
Of light in pitiless armament arrayed!
Pure I reflect you, to your primal place:
See yourself! But to reflect the light
Still presumes a sombre half of shade.

O for myself, alone, within myself,
Beside a heart, at the well-springs of the poem,
Between the void and the supreme event,
I wait the echo of my inner depths,
Bitter, sombre, and sonorous cistern,
Sounding of further depths within the soul.

Do you know, illusory captive of the leaves,
Gulf that feeds on these lean lattices,
Dazzling secrets, over my closed eyes,
What body drags me to its idle end?
What brow draws me to this bony ground?
A spark, there, thinks of my absent ones.

Shut, sacred, filled with insubstantial fire,
Terrestrial fragment offered to the light,
This place delights me, ruled over by torches,
Composed of gold, of stone, of sombre trees,
Where so much marble trembles on so many shadows.
The faithful sea sleeps there, upon my graves.

Resplendent hound, keep off the idolater!
When I, alone, and with a shepherd's smile
For long let pasture these mysterious sheep
And tend the white flock of my quiet tombs,
Keep at a far remove the prudent doves,
The vain deluding dreams, the curious angels.

Now I am here, the future is indolence.
The clean insect scratches at the dryness;
All's burned, undone, resolved within this air
Into what austere essence, who shall say?
Life is vast, being drunk with absentness,
And bitterness is sweet, and the mind clear.

The hidden dead fare well within this earth,
Which warms them, and which dries their mystery.
Noon above, the high motionless Noon,
In itself thinks itself, itself sufficing.
Complete head, and perfect diadem,
I am the secret change at work in you.

You have me only, to contain your fears:
My repentances, my doubtings, my constraints
Are the defect of your great diamond.
But slowly in their marble-heavy night

A shadowy people at the roots of trees
Have ranged themselves already on your side.

They have melted to impenetrable absence,
The red clay has drunk the kindred white,
The gift of life has passed into the flowers.
Where are the well-known phrases of the dead,
The personal ways, the individual souls?
The larva threads where once the teardrops formed.

The sharp cries of girls teased into love,
The eyes, the teeth, the eyelids glistening wet,
The charming breast at dalliance with fire,
The blood that glows upon the yielding lips,
The ultimate gifts, the fingers that defend them,
Go underground, reverting to the game.

And you, great soul, will you await a dream
Free, at last, of these deceitful hues
Contrived for fleshly eyes by wave and gold?
Shall you sing, when you are vaporous?
Come, now! All flows; the clay of flesh is porous;
The holy impatience perishes as well.

Gaunt immortality, in black and gilt,
Hideously laurelled comfortress
Depicting death as a maternal breast
—The flattering falsehood and the pious ruse!
Who does not know, and who does not refuse
This empty skull and this eternal laugh?

Deep-buried fathers, heads untenanted,
Who weighted by such shovelfuls of earth

Are earth at last, and who confuse our paths,
The true devourer, the irrefutable worm,
Is not for you asleep beneath the board,
He lives on life, he does not ever leave me.

Love, perhaps, or hatred of myself?
His secret fang is near to me, so near
That any name might be a fitting one;
What of that? He sees, desires, dreams, touches;
My flesh delights him; even in my bed
I live as something which that being owns.

Zeno, cruel Zeno of Elea,
You have transfixed me with that wingèd arrow
Which quivers, and which flies and does not fly.
The sound begets me, and the arrow kills.
Ah, the sun. . . . What tortoise-shadow for the soul,
Achilles motionless in his great strides!

No, no—up! Enter the time to be,
Break, my body, from this pensive pose,
Drink, my breast, the new birth of the wind.
A freshness, exhaled out of the sea,
Returns my soul to me. O salty power!
Run to the wave, burst forth again, alive!

Yes, great sea endowed with wild delight,
Panther-skin and chlamys pierced and pierced
With myriad and myriad idols of the sun,
Absolute Hydra, drunk with your blue flesh,
You who bite again your sparkling tail
In tumult, though that tumult is like silence,

The wind is rising! One must try to live;
The immense air opens and shuts my book;
The wave dares burst in powder from the rocks.
Take your flight, fly off, all-dazzled pages!
Break, waves! Break with joyous waters
This quiet roof, where sails were foraging.

# The Voice

I was mortal, like the mortal year;
A voice cried out amid the mortal night,
"The year shall suffer the scourges of the wind,
  Mockery of brambles and of thorns,
  Gallows of trees, and sepulchre of ice,
  And this shall be, or the burning wheel of worlds shall break.

"And the burning wheel of worlds shall break but it shall be
  That graves shall crack and the dead issue like mist,
  Like mist ascend, and put on rainbow raiment,
  And the choirs of blossoms assemble again in glory,
  And the tall angel of the lily
  Trumpet to the sun the fragrance of risen spring."

## Poet to Reader

### I

"The cowboy saw the sagebrush-land as sea.
There, in the dusk, a ghostly ocean raged,
The waves rolled, and the shadows of the waves,
The twilight glistened on the rushing foam.
And in a twilight half a world away
A sailor leaned above the herded waves,
The ghostly plains resounded with their cries,
The twilight glistened on their horns of foam."

### II

In silence, in the silent room, you read
These words I wrote in silence, in a silent room.
There is no voice, and yet you hear a voice
Which does not speak, and which you cannot hear.
Out of a placeless Place the silent speech
Echoes in silence in a timeless Time
And sea is changed to plain, and plain to sea,
And one world fades, another comes to be.

What shall I build you with these syllables
Of voiceless voice, made out of breath unbreathed?
My power is momentary, and endures
Only for one moment without end,
Yet for that moment I am Prospero,
Our minds move to one music, and are one,
I can do all, and build all as you will.

### III

O luminous worlds within the twilight brain!
These phantasms are phantasms, but true
As dreams are true within the dreaming mind.
Suppose the imagination could devise
Not visionary but substantial things,

Do these not also perish? Shall we weave
Immortal garlands out of mortal blooms,
Build changeless palaces of melting snows?

The statue is shaped within the sculptor's brain;
Hence it is not the marble nor the bronze,
Though bronze and marble manifest to sense
What else were imperceptible. Thus, once made,
It cannot be unmade. Though stone be shattered
Or metal melted, Form survives the formed,
In placeless Place and timeless Time of thought.
Although no longer manifest, it Is.
We make the imperishable of perishing things.

## IV

Perhaps all tales of suffering gods are only
Legends of the resurrected spring,
Parables of the grain that must be cut,
The grape that must be crushed, for bread and wine:
The death of life, that other life may live.
Do we doubt divinity, ourselves divine?
It does not matter. Let the petals fall,
Let the snows vanish, and the seasons change:
Here are unfading flowers, unmelting snows.

The immortal wreath must mock the mortal brow,
But these eternals are as brief as we.
We gaze from celestial portals, and behold
How one world fades, another comes to be.
Our moment is a moment, yet it holds
World after luminous world, as we might see
All starry heaven in one drop of dew:
Worlds bodiless as such mirrored stars, but bright,
And yours and mine in perpetuity.